Praise for

SEVEN SPRINGS: A MEMOIR

by Ellen Blum Barish

"In her new memoir, *Seven Springs*, Ell... explores big questions about what makes a ... one does so in two compelling narrative threads: one examining a car accident that occurred when she was a girl, and the aftermath of that experience; the other delving into the underpinnings of her faith life and how that faith informs her relationships and her place in the world. When she becomes a mother, she engages the tradition. The fruit of that study informs this memoir. 'Judaism,' Barish observes, 'is by its very nature an ongoing conversation.' That conversation, which she joins and shares, enriches this absorbing story."

—RICK BAILEY, author of *Get Thee to a Bakery, The Enjoy Agenda, Italian Chocolate*, and *American English*

"In lyrical prose and with the sensibility of a reporter on a mission, Ellen Blum Barish begins an excavation of her life that leads her back, again and again, to the car accident she survived as a child. . . . This memoir is an exploration of family, friendship and faith, and of what happens when we find our voices after too many years of being silenced. This is a beautiful book, both familiar and surprising, and Ellen Blum Barish is a beautiful writer. *Seven Springs* is a gift that will invite any reader to see his or her own past with a fresh perspective."

—KATE HOPPER, author of *Ready for Air: A Journey Through Premature Motherhood* and *Use Your Words: A Writing Guide for Mothers*

"A thoughtful meditation on the nature of trauma, memory, and Judaism. In *Seven Springs*, Ellen Blum Barish illustrates how shared experiences stamp each life in a unique way. This inspiring work calls upon readers to be introspective and assemble the puzzle pieces of their own lives."

—FERN SCHUMER CHAPMAN, author of *Brothers, Sisters, Strangers; Motherland;* and *Is It Night or Day?*

"The truths that Ellen finds through her own brave journey are truths that resonate for all of us. . . . She roots her reader in scenes that are rendered so exquisitely we become conjoined in her discovery. . . . Ellen's writing holds the power to open hearts and minds, and leave us all with deeper understandings of ourselves and our place in this world."

—BARBARA MAHANY, author of *The Stillness of Winter, Slowing Time: Seeing the Sacred Outside Your Kitchen Door, The Blessings of Motherprayer: Sacred Whispers of Mothering*, and *Motherprayer: Lessons in Loving*

"Ellen Blum Barish brings real life to life with a strong sense of narrative, the unswerving observation of a reporter, and an abiding commitment to meanings that run deep. She hones in on day-to-day experiences and won't let us go until we see the connectedness she's found, the underlying causes we might have missed, the richness that is in us and in our relationships."

—LEE REILLY, author of *Teaching Maggie* and *Women Living Single*

"Excavating memory, Ellen Blum Barish circles back through personal history to make sense of silence—that is imposed upon us, and how we can finally trust ourselves to speak. An intricate investigation of the past, exploring how we might reach back in time to change our present."

—ALLISON K. WILLIAMS, author of *Seven Drafts: Self-Edit Like a Pro From Blank Page to Book*

SEVEN SPRINGS

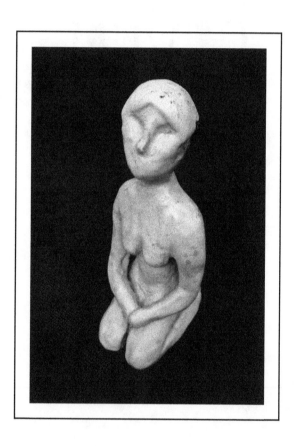

SEVEN SPRINGS

A MEMOIR

What a season can reveal...

ELLEN BLUM BARISH

Ellen Blum Barish

SHANTI ARTS PUBLISHING
BRUNSWICK, MAINE

SEVEN SPRINGS

A MEMOIR

Published by Shanti Arts Publishing
Interior and cover design by Shanti Arts Designs

Shanti Arts LLC
193 Hillside Road
Brunswick, Maine 04011
shantiarts.com

Cover photo of the author, 1968. Frontispiece
photo of the figurine made by the author,
circa 1974. Both used with permission.

Dr. Rachel Naomi Remen's quote is from the *On Being
with Krista Tippett* podcast that aired August 11, 2005.

This book is a memoir. To protect privacy, some
names and characteristics of individuals have been
changed. The events and conversations recounted in
this book come from the author's best recollections
and are presented in a way that evokes the feeling
and meaning of the experience at that time.

ISBN: 978-1-951651-82-4 (softcover)
ISBN: 978-1-951651-83-1 (ebook)

Library of Congress Control Number: 2021936749

For JWH

Also by Ellen Blum Barish

Views from the Home Office Window:
On Motherhood, Family and Life
(Adams Street Publishing, 2007)

From the heart of the holy darkness emerged a great ray of light. And then, perhaps because this is a Jewish story, there was an accident, and the vessels containing the light of the world, the wholeness of the world, broke. And the wholeness of the world, the light of the world was scattered into a thousand thousand fragments of light, and they fell into all events and all people, where they remain deeply hidden until this very day. Now, according to my grandfather, the whole human race is a response to this accident. We are here because we are born with the capacity to find the hidden light in all events and all people, to lift it up and make it visible once again and thereby to restore the innate wholeness of the world. It's a very important story for our times. And this task is called *tikkun olam* in Hebrew. It's the restoration of the world.

—Naomi Rachel Remen

CONTENTS

ACKNOWLEDGMENTS

MANUSCRIPTS DON'T BECOME BOOKS WITHOUT THE EYES, ears, and heart of human beings with a connection to the writer or the material. My profound gratitude goes to Christine Cote at Shanti Arts who resonated with Seven Springs and felt it worthy of her time and her publishing company's catalogue.

To the editors, publishers, and producers who connected with the story as a seedling and gave it water and air. Rebecca Harris and Collette Jacobs, the publishers at Adams Street Publishing who granted me newspaper space for a version of this story's first print appearance. Cate Cahan gave it voice when she green-lighted a different version for a Chicago Public Radio commentary. Belinda Lichty Clarke encouraged me to expand it in a longer form for *Medill Magazine*. Jill Howe put me and a version of the story in her Story Sessions lineup on stage. Jeremy Owens invited me to tell a story from the book at *You're Being Ridiculous*, and I shared the first chapter at Scott Whitehair's solo show, *Fresh Meat*.

I will forever be grateful to Jill Pollack for hiring me to teach writing at Story Studio Chicago, introducing me to Ragdale, and writing a recommendation for a residency there that gifted me with the time to transform twenty pages into the first draft of this book.

To the writers who lent their literary sensibilities to early drafts—Lee Strickland, Becky Talbot, Barbara Mahany, Lee Reilly, Megan Wells, the writers of Friends with Words—as well as Felicia Eth and Anne Edelstein, who offered insightful feedback, my deepest appreciation. I made enormous progress one fall weekend at Roberta Levin's Wisconsin home and so appreciated her thoughtful notes and am grateful for the publishing conversations I had with Nina Barrett, Judith Matz, Pam Zbesko, Kacky Solley, and Gail Conway. Miriam Bauer provided the book with a thoughtful continuity reading, and Nancy Liskar gave it a sharp-eyed proofreading.

The memoir would not have made it to the page without the deep and insightful editorial exchanges with Kate Hopper that not only improved the writing but encouraged and inspired me to persevere, especially during the proposal writing and selling process. And a huge shout out to Allison K. Williams, Ashleigh Renard, and The Writer's Bridge for the great gift of writerly community building and wisdom on book promotion.

Digging around in traumatic memory can be a high-risk endeavor, and I am indebted to the healers and wise ones who kept me physically, psychologically, and spiritually stable: Dr. Paul Kentor, Dr. Anne Niedenthal, Marsha Warren, Roseann Martarano, Debbie Kristofek, Marsha Richman, Renee Cortez, Leslie McGuirk, my Her Chapter compatriots, my SoulSpace sisters, Rabbi Andrea London, Rabbi Peter Knobel, Rabbi Eleanor Smith, Marci Dickman, and Hyma Levin.

The title for the book came when I was sitting in the red velvet chair that my brilliant and beautiful friend Mary Ellen Sullivan bequeathed to me, and I felt her magnificent hummingbird presence during so many writing sessions.

Finally, to my nearest and dearest who have the misfortune to have a memoirist as a family member or friend, my seatmates in the accident, Jennifer West Hawksworth, Caroline West, and Sally West (in memoriam); and treasured friends, Alysse Einbender, Marianne Mitchell, and Sean Rosemeyer, my unending love. And this book would probably still be under construction if it wasn't for the deep well of strength and support that is my bashert, my beloved David. I carry each of these human beings inside of me, and the stories we lived together have left their imprint on my soul. This book is my expression of love and appreciation for the divine mystery, my soul's offering.

Ellen Blum Barish
April 2021

PROLOGUE

EVERY YEAR BETWEEN MARCH AND MAY, I FEEL A TUG pulling me to the East. The pink and white dogwood trees, yellow forsythia bushes, and purple and red azaleas that bloom psychedelically in Philadelphia's spring lure. I long to leave the Midwest's bone-chilling landscape of gray that can hang on as late as June.

And so I go.

Returning to my hometown in spring has kept me close to family members and my two best friends from high school. Making those trips has allowed me to revisit the gravel paths of Fairmont Park, Valley Green, and the Wissahickon and wait in long lines for corned beef sandwiches at Fourth Street Deli, cheesesteaks at Dalessandro's, and soft pretzels on city street corners.

But prior to every trip, in the midst of preparing and packing, I feel a tinge of foreboding, electrical activity in my nervous system that I previously chose to think of as excitement. Now I understand it as my body's association with a place where a terrible thing happened. On an April afternoon when I was twelve, a Mack truck sped through the intersection of Carpenter Lane and McCallum Street and collided with the Volkswagen station wagon that was taking me and two others home from school. Mere seconds shattered our realities, followed by decades of deafening silence.

When something that big and loud is covered with a blanket of quiet, it lies there, appearing as protection. But instead, it can be heavy and immobilizing, impacting us in ways we may come to know, and many we won't. After the accident, I went numb. I buried the memory, and blindly carried its weight until a conversation at my twentieth high school reunion broke the silence, returning me to my past, to myself, and to something I now understand as faith.

REMEMBERING

Forgetfulness leads to exile, while remembrance is the secret of redemption.

—Baal Shem Tov

SPRING 1997

I WAS STANDING BY THE DOUBLE DOORS AT THE ENTRANCE of our former high school considering a quick exit when I saw her. The moment our eyes met, hers twinkled just as I remembered them when we were twelve. They took me right back to that afternoon in her basement when we danced to every single track from *Tommy* by The Who, leaping from the couch to the floor and back again, dripping with sweat, all adrenalin and giggles.

It was mid-May and threat of rain had moved the reunion picnic inside to the front hall where a handful of our former classmates were talking in small groups. Prominent Quaker alumni eyed us from their portraits on the wall. I was solo, but not by design. My husband, David, had opted out of this one, choosing to stay in Chicago with our two daughters over chit-chatting with people he had never met nor would probably ever see again. I was disappointed until it occurred to me that his decision offered me the rare chance to hang out with my two best friends from high school and allow him some time alone with his girls.

But my two best friends weren't there. Alysse's son had a soccer game and Marianne was at the hospital with her mother who had taken a fall. Though Marianne was hosting the evening reunion party and I'd see them later, I was getting antsy to leave.

I was strategizing a quick escape when I saw her standing by the wall, scanning, as I was, for someone to talk to. I hadn't laid eyes on Jenny in twenty years, since we sat on folding chairs in white sundresses holding white carnations on the front steps of this building for our graduation photograph. Two children were arranging puzzle pieces at her feet.

As I approached her, she smiled wistfully and her eyes dimmed, and suddenly, I was drawing a blank about the last time we spoke. Ours was a small class, about seventy altogether, and though Jenny and I became friends in seventh grade as new girls at school and stayed classmates through senior year, I couldn't remember us having a single conversation during our high school years.

That's when, standing just a few inches from her, I heard myself blurt, "Jenny! How are you?" at a higher pitch than I intended.

"I've been okay," she said, in a friendly but measured tone. "These are my kids." She glanced down at a girl about fourteen and a boy I guessed to be ten. "They're already getting bored, though. I might just take them home early."

We were in our late thirties and our faces had changed shape since senior year. Mine was a good bit plumper, but she was still freckled and fair skinned, like me. Her hair still light brown, like mine.

We exchanged post-graduation headlines. After college, she returned to Philadelphia and worked as a bookkeeper at a small business. She had two children and was recently divorced. I told her about my work as a journalist in Chicago and that I had remained in the Midwest after college, which was where my husband was now.

"He's at home with our daughters," I told her. "Emily is nine and our five-year-old is named Jenny."

"Good choice," she said, and her lips curled into a soft smile that broke out into a chuckle. Oh, that laugh! Instantly,

I remembered how Jenny could cross her eyes or tangle up her lips, prompting me to mirror her because I could. How quickly things with her could skew silly and become infectious.

We sank into a long pause, regarding one another. The silence was lengthening, and suddenly, I began to feel incredibly anxious. My molars were bearing down and my jaw began to tighten.

Just a few weeks before the reunion, the tooth and jaw pain I had been wrestling with for most of my life had become so agonizing that my dentist had talked me into a pricey, hard-plastic mouth guard to save the surface of my teeth from the force of my own grinding. But wearing it at night didn't do a damn thing in the daytime. When I got nervous, my mouth became a wild animal, my teeth bearing down like a lion protecting her kill. Standing in front of Jenny, eye to eye now, electrical activity began whizzing in my head, and suddenly, I made a connection.

Mouth pain. Car accident.

That's when a question that would send me on a twenty-year journey erupted, without my consent.

"Jenny, do you remember the accident?"

In the spring of 1972, I was twelve and Jenny had just turned thirteen. We were in the back seat of her mother's Volkswagen station wagon on a ride home from school that ended in a collision with a Mack truck. Her mother was driving. Her older sister, Caroline, was in the front passenger seat. I sat behind Caroline in the back passenger seat. None of us were buckled.

That much I remembered. But I didn't remember details or ever talking with Jenny or anyone else about it afterward.

Her expression shifted. Her eyes went glassy and distant. I was usually more sensitive. My question had come out of nowhere.

I had been so close to hightailing it out of there.

Her daughter and son scrambled up from the floor, and she introduced me. Without taking her eyes from mine, her daughter asked, "Mom, is this the Ellen from the accident?" Jenny nodded and her children inspected me. I felt the intensity of their collective stares. "The accident," her daughter had said, as if the words were in capital letters.

A chill shook my neck and shoulders, but Jenny wasn't walking away just yet.

It occurred to me that my question may have sounded nonchalant, so I clarified.

"I have very little memory about that day," I offered.

"I remember almost everything, if you want to hear," she replied.

I didn't know how to respond because I didn't know how I felt. I am frequently unsure about how to assess a situation until long after an event is over and I have had a chance to think or write about it. I get quiet in the midst of something new or something I sense to be big, expert in stilling my breath and body so I can be present, but inside, I go numb. Later, long after, I can name the sensation. I often operate in a sphere of delayed-response, feelings just out of reach as if they are floating on the unprotected side of a bubble.

Something in her eyes struck me as pleading, as if she needed to talk about it too, as if the subject itself wanted air.

"Sure," I said. But it sounded more like a question.

"We were talking about Leslie's bat mitzvah." I was amazed that twenty-five years later Jenny remembered what we were talking about moments before the impact. She said the words as if she were reporting facts she had repeated many times before. Her children had returned to their puzzling on the hall rug.

"You were saying that Leslie was planning her bat mitzvah, and at that very moment we were passing her house. I remember turning to look out the back of the car just as we stopped at the red light at the intersection. The light turned green, and I turned around to sit down. Then we entered the intersection and that's when the truck careened through and hit us on the front passenger side."

"Oh, God. That I remember."

"There were two impacts," she said. "The first was in the

intersection, but the force of it sent us toward a parked car on the other side of the street. That did most of the damage."

I didn't remember that. How could I not remember that?

"I was flung over the driver's seat and had a concussion. My mother had multiple serious injuries."

I remembered seeing her mother in profile in the driver's seat from where I was sitting, the dashboard at her waist. Many months later, I saw her mother at school in a wheelchair.

"She died from complications of her injuries fifteen and a half years later."

I stared into her eyes, stunned.

How did I not know this? How could I have known so little about the gravity of her injuries, and her mother's, about what happened after the crash?

"Oh, God. Jenny, I had no idea."

She nodded solemnly, acknowledging. Her children were starting to fidget, but she continued.

"Caroline got stitches in her knee and her tooth was chipped."

I hadn't recalled that either. My head began to spin, trying to square these details with the few I did know, which mainly consisted of the sight of Jenny pressed against the back seat, eyes closed, mouth open, her back slightly arched. I would never unsee that in my mind's eye.

"I knew you had a severe head injury, and I later learned you had gone into a coma."

"Yep," she said, without any change in her expression or tone of voice. "I had a concussion, four broken ribs, and amnesia. I had to relearn how to walk and talk. I found out later that the doctors had initially given me a 20 percent chance of survival." She was as committed to recounting the facts as I was when reporting a story, listing the details as if they were someone else's, a quality that probably served her as well in her bookkeeping as it did for me as a reporter. But as I took them in, I could feel myself leaving my body.

"I remember hearing your voice just as I was fighting to remain conscious. You cried out, 'Jenny's dead!'"

I swallowed hard. Behind me, I could hear whoops of laughter and the buzz of conversation as our former classmates chatted about their jobs, children, divorces, or changes on campus.

"I remember wanting to say, 'I'm not dead! I just can't talk! Or move!'"

I stood, motionless, staring into her eyes.

She asked, "Your tooth was knocked out, right?"

"Yes." I turned my gaze down to break the spell. I remembered that my face had been pressed, hard, into the leather seatback at the moment of impact—I'm not sure if it was the first or second, but when I pulled away from it, my mouth was dripping with blood and I had lost my front tooth.

Jenny and I shared the back seat during a horrible crash that afternoon, and her entire life changed that day. And I had just lost a tooth.

"We had a lot of tough times, Ellen, but we're survivors. Hopefully, stronger and better for it." She smiled, and I was overcome with the memory of her thoughtfulness, positivity, and graciousness. How had I lost touch with such a sweet and tender soul?

"Well, I should get these kids home. It was nice talking with you."

I nodded and watched as she turned toward the doors with her children and entered the vestibule. It was drizzling now, but something made me run after her.

"Would you be open to talking about this more? Over the phone?"

"Sure," she said, and she softly held my eyes with hers. She wanted to continue this conversation too. I handed her the back of a check deposit slip, the only paper I could find in my pocketbook, and I grabbed a pen from the front hall desk. She scribbled her phone number, and I watched as she made her way through the doors.

As I saw her step into the street, I felt faint and reached for the nearest hard surface, the edge of the front hall wooden counter where Mrs. Bristol would sit by her switchboard to call our parents when we were sick and needed to be picked up from school.

I hadn't just walked away from a car accident that spring day in 1972. I had walked away from a friend—a girl whose name I unconsciously chose for one of my daughters—and I had packed away my memory of it and shoved it far back on a shelf.

Were the things she told me things I used to know but forgot? Or things I just couldn't bring myself to remember?

•

The night of the reunion party there was a good crowd at Marianne's. Maybe thirty-five or forty, a decent turnout for our small class. Jenny wasn't there. I had been so shaken by our conversation that I didn't think to ask if she was planning to come. But she hadn't been a big partygoer in school, so I wasn't really surprised. After everyone left, Alysse and I stayed to help clean up. Since Alysse and Marianne were living in Philadelphia and I was in Chicago, all of us working, married, with small children, it was rare for all three of us to connect beyond short, interrupted phone calls and email. It was my first chance to tell them about my conversation with Jenny that afternoon. Even after several glasses of wine, I was still vibrating.

"Hey, you guys. I need to tell you what happened at the picnic," I said, finding my moment.

Marianne turned off the faucet, grabbed a glass and what was left of the wine, and pulled a chair to the table.

When I needed them, they were there.

"I know it was decades ago, but why can't I remember so many of the details from something as awful as this? Do you remember anything?" I searched Alysse's eyes, drowsy from wine and the day.

"I remember an assembly." Marianne remembered

everything. Dates. Weather. What people wore, especially the color.

"We knew there was an accident," she said, her eyes piercing mine. "That it was serious but you were home and safe, and Jenny, Caroline, and their mother were in the hospital. But that you were fine."

"Did we talk over the weekend? Did you know about my tooth? Did I tell you anything?"

"I didn't know about your tooth until later." She looked at me, then at Alysse. "But it probably would have been difficult to talk over the weekend with a missing tooth and bleeding mouth." Marianne was an abstract painter, but she was exceptionally practical, brimming with common sense. I knew they could see my struggle to piece this together, but they were also mystified by my questions. Their eyes saying, what's the big deal?

"You didn't say a word about it," Alysse offered. "It just didn't seem like a big thing to you, so it wasn't for us. We thought you were lucky."

Lucky. Yes. I was lucky. Incredibly. But what was gnawing at me was what could have possibly kept me from talking about being hit by a Mack truck with my two best friends? Even stranger, what could have kept me from talking about it with the girl with whom I shared the experience?

I picked up my wine glass and tipped it for Alysse to pour me one more.

●

I was in the guest bedroom at my father's house, where I had been staying for the weekend, when I found it. It was my last morning in Philadelphia.

My dad was living with his wife, Frances, in a house on the edge of Fairmont Park just a few blocks from my childhood home. The morning after the reunion, I reached for my reading glasses that I had left on a shelf, and behind a hockey trophy belonging to one of Fran's sons I saw it: a clay sculpture of a female nude that I had made in ninth grade. It was about seven inches high, glazed in a peachy tone, head tilted slightly, hair up in a bun, kneeling on both knees.

We were sophomores in high school when Alysse discovered her gift for sculpture. Marianne's painting talent had already revealed itself a few years before. I felt like there was an artist inside of me—I wanted to have an artist inside of me—but I was still searching for what that could be. There were too many decisions to make in painting—too many choices for canvases, colors, and brush types—but the tactile, malleable nature of clay appealed and persuaded me to choose it.

A small section of her hair had chipped and fallen into something cobalt blue and then glued back on—you could see the thick, zigzagging crack on the side of her head—and she had delicate, sloping shoulders, perky breast buds, and tiny, mitten-shaped hands.

Her proportions were off, but there was something innocent about her. It wasn't just about her being naked. It was the tilt of her head. Her slender shoulders. Her broken bun. She was something that remained of my childhood in my father's house, and I wanted to take her home with me. After their divorce, my parents sold our home, and many of my childhood belongings had been tossed. I had so few objects from my past, and I wanted her. So at breakfast, after Fran left for a run, I poured coffee and half-and-half into a mug, sat down at the table where my father was reading, and asked him if I could take the figurine back with me to Chicago.

"Sure," he said, his hand on his coffee, eyes on *The Wall Street Journal*.

I wanted him to acknowledge this little piece of me from my childhood, at the very least to ask to see it. I waited for him to look up for just a moment of attention on this small thing because to see it would mean that he was seeing me. But a high school art object didn't quite compete with the business pages.

•

Back in Chicago, I pored over every one of my journals, scouring for a hint or mention of the accident. I was a dutiful diarist with piles of notebooks, close to forty—black cardboard sketchbooks, composition books, leather, fabric, watermarked, lined, lineless, bound, and hard-backed journals—that I have kept since I was thirteen. I paged through every entry, word, scribble, quote, and doodle. I had marked important dates, starts and ends to high school friendships, guest lists of parties, and snippets of quotes from family arguments. There were accounts of affection from boyfriends, and lack of it, as well as insufferably long sections of self-analysis and a heavy reliance on Hugh Prather quotes calligraphed over entire pages. But there wasn't a single clue, not a change of pen color, or shaky hand, or letters in code to suggest that something very big had happened, that everything had changed one afternoon on a ride home from school, that I had come so close to the sharp edge of death.

It took weeks to go through my journals. I was determined to find some detail, some piece of information written in my own hand at the time that I could trust to jog my memory or help me understand what happened after.

I found nothing. I set the pages aside and tried to remember. I couldn't conjure the moment of impact. I didn't see the truck coming, even though it hit us on the passenger side where Caroline and I were seated. My attention was on Jenny and our conversation. All I could recall was the gagging sensation from the blood coagulating in my mouth after my face hit that leather seatback. My mouth was muffled in that seatback, taking my breath and ability to shriek or wail or cry. Now I was lost in a maze of muddy memories, unable to latch on to any one concrete moment or feeling.

•

A few weeks after the reunion, in my bedroom in Chicago, I unwrapped the clay statuette that had been rolled up in a t-shirt in the corner of my closet and showed it to my husband.

He looked at the sculpture, then at me with his blue-gray eyes, smiled and said, "Wow. Nice."

David wasn't a gusher. His approval of this thing I'd made pleased me.

I placed the little figurine ceremoniously on the dresser. I was surprised at how weighty and substantial she was for her size. Her delicate frame clearly a representation of young me at fourteen or fifteen, fired in clay. I pulled her closer and inspected her for the first time since I had hurriedly removed her from the shelf at my father's house. I wanted to look at her as art, more critically. Except for the mitten hands that gave her a cartoonish quality, the rest of her was rather realistic. Not half bad for a young girl, an artist wannabe. There was something lovely about the tilt of her head, the thoughtfulness in the indentation of her eyes, and the accuracy of her nose. But when my eyes dropped below her nose, what I saw sent electricity through my jaw. Rather, what I didn't see. The bottom half of her face was completely smooth. She had no lips, no teeth. Not a dimple or dent. Not a scratch or line. Just a flat surface of solid clay skin.

A mouth fired shut.

BREAKING

And just as a seed cannot grow to
perfection [without] decomposition,
so these points [of light] could not
become perfect configurations as
long as they maintained their original
form, but only by shattering.

—Menahem Azaria of Fano

SPRING 1972

THE HOUSE I GREW UP IN WASN'T A GO-TO. MY PARENTS
weren't big social hosts or keen on my brother and I inviting
friends over. My father, like so many working fathers of his
time, wasn't around much. He worked long hours, and my
mother liked things quiet and clean. She had a deep aversion
to blood, dirt, and broken glass.

But by the time I was in seventh grade, my mother had
become swept up in the women's movement and was building
a career. Still, she was the primary caretaker of our house,
my brother, and me, and needed to keep things in order.
Guests were, for the most part, not very welcome.

Adding to all of this was her anxiety around messiness.
Whenever a ceramic plate or drinking glass broke in our
house or my brother or I would track dirt or mud in from
outside, her body would freeze. Once she pulled herself
together, she'd put on rubber gloves, send us out of the room,
and sweep it up, unless my father was around and she could
get him to do it, insisting that we steer clear of the spot until,
I don't know, any remaining particles disintegrated into the
floor?

My mother came by her dedication to spotlessness
epigenetically. She spent the bulk of her childhood living
in a rented hotel room as the only child of an obsessive-

compulsive, white-glove-wearing, hospital-corner-making, dirt-averse Jewish mother. *A hotel.* Though she lived in Pittsburgh rather than at the Plaza, I pictured her as Eloise before Eloise was Eloise—immaculate version—eating her breakfast in the hotel dining room where the kitchen staff made her peanut butter and jelly sandwiches to take to school for lunch. It was supposed to be temporary while they looked for a house, but they lived there for almost ten years. As a result, a tidy, institutionally decorated hotel room was my mother's idea of home.

Her father, my Grandpa Reuben, was a word-game-loving restaurant supply store wholesaler who was, like my father, rarely home. I saw her parents only a handful of times in my life because their disinclination for driving and flying kept them in Pittsburgh. I still carry around this vision of my Grandma Ruth standing over us during a visit to her apartment, not quite sitting or standing, in a sort of ready position, hovering. As if she was in a constant state of preparing to flee.

Not surprising that with at least two generations of anxiety woven into my family tree, my mother's worries felt like my own.

There was also great ambivalence, on both of my parents' part about being Jewish. Both of my parents were Jewish on both sides, going back generations. I am 99.8 percent Eastern European Ashkenazi Jewish—German on my dad's side and Russian on my mother's. All four of my grandparents were Jewish, although in a decision that I think of as the seedling of my mother's disinterest in her heritage, her mother legally changed her own name from Rose to Ruth so it wouldn't sound "so ethnic."

If asked, my parents would say they considered themselves Reform Jews, but in the loosest sense of the words. Neither was interested in ritual or tradition or their Jewish roots. There wasn't a single prayer book or Shabbat candle or anything with a Hebrew letter anywhere in the house I grew up in. We were not synagogue members,

Sukkah builders, or hosts for holiday gatherings on Passover, Rosh Hashanah, or Hanukkah. I don't recall ever walking into a synagogue with either of my parents. The only spiritual book I ever saw in the house was Kahlil Gibran's *The Prophet*.

Their goal, like many Jews who grew up after World War II, was assimilation. The mission was to fit in. For Jews like my father's father, my Grandpa Kurt who emigrated from Germany just before the war, there were complicated feelings around being Jewish. There was a combination of relief at landing safely in the United States mixed in with some guilt about surviving.

Though she grew up with no siblings or cousins and lived primarily in a grown-up environment, my mother's childhood was generally happy. She went to overnight camp in the summers, and her parents sent her to a fancy private school for girls. Until the day of the accident, I believe no event in my mother's lifetime had ever been that chaotic. Her only daughter was in a terrible car wreck. On her way home from school. Driven home by another mother whom she didn't know. The accident turned her world upside down.

It was different for me. During the crash, I left my body. I was there and not there at the same time, which would become a pattern in my life. Bewildered, but not in any noticeable pain. By the time the police and ambulances arrived, my mind was overcome with worry over how my mother was going to feel.

Because my mother's worries worried me.

I don't remember what happened at the hospital, but I do remember that on the drive home that afternoon, we rode in silence. Mom wouldn't look at me. That was how she was handling this. If she didn't give it too much thought, it might just go away. It was dinnertime when we got back home, but my mother walked past the kitchen and started up the stairs to the second floor.

"I'm going to check on Adam," she said to the air as she

walked into my younger brother's room. "Go on to your room, El. Just keep your head upright and try to stay still."

I didn't want to go to my bedroom. I was bleeding. What about all this blood? I didn't want to be alone. How was I going to sleep? I wanted to know what was happening to Jenny and Caroline and their mother. Why wouldn't Mom tell me anything?

I stood in the hallway and watched as she picked up the dirty clothes in Adam's room and gently kissed his forehead. When she reentered the hall, she sighed and walked toward her bedroom.

At her door, she said, without turning around, "You need to rest. Now please go to your room," and her door closed with a soft click.

I was used to my mother needing her privacy. She spent a lot of time in her bedroom, mostly on her bed, where she wrote checks, turned down the corners on articles in *Ms.* magazine and filed her nails, painting them with pale pink polish. But she usually left her door open, at least a crack.

I wanted her to hold me, to tell me everything was going to be alright.

Hot tears ran down my cheeks.

In my room, I tried to find a comfortable position. As it soaked up more blood, the gauze that was wedged in between my teeth kept changing shape. I had to rearrange it. It got all gummy and I couldn't swallow, so I took it out. But when I saw that moist red blob in my fingers, my throat went dry and stiff; I felt like I was going to gag. I slid off the bed and ran to the bathroom just as clumps of vomit exploded from my mouth onto the floor. I found the nearest towel to wipe it up. Lucky, I thought, that none of it got on my blue-and-pink-flowered Marimekko bedspread.

When I got back to my bed, I leaned against the wall, put a new square of gauze in my mouth, and propped up a few pillows so I could rest my arm. Mom had said to stay still. I held my position and my breath and heard my heart pound-pound, pound-pound. I could see my chest moving.

The house was really quiet. I thought about getting up to see what Adam was doing, but I didn't want to upset him. It was becoming clear I was going to have to bear this alone.

I looked at the clock. Seven. Why didn't Mom make dinner? It would have been hard for me to eat, but I was hungry. I wondered what Jenny was doing. And Caroline. And their mom. One minute we were on McCallum Street on our way home from school, and the next our car was on the other side of the street, my mouth bleeding and Jenny's eyes closed.

After what felt like hours, shifting from half-sitting to half-lying positions on my bed, changing the gauze every few minutes, and my head racing with thoughts, I heard the front door slam. Dad was home. I heard him clomp up the stairs. He wasn't a big man, but he made his presence known. He had big energy, explosive energy, especially when he was angry, and it frightened me so much that I never wanted to be the cause of it. He knocked on my door and without waiting for a reply, opened it.

After inspecting me from the doorway, he furrowed his bushy jet-black eyebrows and said, "You're fine. You'll be fine." It sounded more like an order. Then he closed the door and headed across the hall to his bedroom and study. In a few minutes, I could smell the aroma of his sweet pipe tobacco and hear Sarah Vaughn's voice crooning from the record player in the den.

The emergency room doctor and my parents said I was fine. That I was lucky it was only a tooth. I really wanted to be fine. But I didn't feel fine.

After what felt like hours with gauze in my mouth and wet cheeks, I heard a knock on my bedroom door. Through the gauze, I mumbled, "Mmmmmm in." It was Grandma Jane, my father's mother, the grandma who lived in town, the one I adored. She opened the door, walked over to the bed, and held me with her deep brown eyes.

"Let's get you into the bath," she said as she took my hand in hers.

My father's parents lived thirty minutes away in the city. My mother must have called her. Grandma Jane had learned to drive late in her life. She rarely drove at night, which was why I was surprised to see her. She rarely visited us in the evening and certainly never alone. But that night she jumped into her white Volkswagen Beetle and drove to our house. I didn't hear the doorbell ring, so she must have let herself into the house with her key.

I was so happy to see her. At just under five feet tall, Grandma Jane was our family's tiny but mighty nurturing heart. She was adoring. Birthday-smothering. A devoted letter writer whose notes to all of her grandchildren at camp, and even at college, frequently included a ten-dollar bill. She remembered that I liked onions *on* my hamburgers, not mixed in. That I liked my Coca-Cola with ginger ale. That I loved chopped chicken liver with Triscuits or Wheat Thins.

Unlike my mother's mother, Grandma Jane embraced being Jewish. She was active in her synagogue's sisterhood, regularly went to High Holy Day services, and had a personal relationship with her rabbi. Hers was the house we gathered in for Passover and Rosh Hashanah.

Grandma Jane led me to the bathroom, where she filled the white porcelain tub with bubble bath up to the rim. She let it run a long time; I had never seen the tub that full. She turned her back while I slid in, and when I turned around to look at her, I saw her kneel on the cold tile floor, fold her skirt under her knees, and run her small fingers through her jet-black hair with the swath of gray in front. I wondered where my mother was, baffled as to why she didn't come to say hello. But with my grandmother there, sitting quietly with me, I was, finally, able to breathe. I was feeling more settled, the calmest I had felt since the accident. She looked back at me with concern, smiling at me with her eyes. We sat there together quietly while she lightly stroked my back, wordlessly, for the longest and most luxurious bath I'd ever had.

After my finger and toe pads were wrinkled, she dried me off with a warm towel, turned the other way as I got into my nightgown, and then escorted me back to my room. She grabbed another pillow from the hall closet, set it on my bed, and waited until I found a comfortable position. Then she slipped back into the night.

Decades later I would discover that my grandmother had cared for me in a way that closely approximated *bikur cholim*, the Jewish etiquette for caring for people who are sick or injured. The guidelines include everything from the length of time for a visit, the time of day, one's body posture to what one wears.

For example, the Talmud states that one should visit during the last three hours of the day when the pain is strongest. My grandmother arrived late in the evening.

The Talmud says that the one who enters to visit the sick should not sit on a bed, nor a bench, nor a chair but should enrobe himself and sit on the ground for the Divine Presence rests above the bed of the patient. Grandma Jane sat on the cold tile bathroom floor at my back and did not hover.

It tells the loved one to dress as if he or she is going to synagogue. Grandma was wearing a dress.

Remain quiet, the Talmud admonishes, as silence is an act of kindness for those who are sick. She didn't say a word. She just stroked my back and listened to me breathe.

Position oneself at the same level as the sick person, says the Talmud, as it is an indication of empathy. Grandma sat on the floor behind me.

And the Talmud states that a visitor should not overstay.

After the bath, she toweled me dry, returned me to my bed, and headed home.

My grandmother's instinct to come to my side in the night by herself was her nature. But showing up and knowing what to do are different things. She must have known that she'd be needed, that perhaps I wouldn't be getting what I needed that dark night of my twelve-year-old soul.

She had a Jewish soul. A Jewishly soaked heart.

I didn't know it then, but that bath and my grandmother's

quiet presence that night constitute the sense memory I carry of what Judaism, and love, look like.

•

Not only were they uninterested in Judaism, my parents had little to no curiosity about God. I remember being seven and asking them what they believed about God. It must have come up in something I read or heard.

So I asked my father if we believed in God, and he told me to ask Mom.

My mother was washing the dinner dishes when I asked. She thought for a moment and said she didn't know, but that there might be something bigger than us out there, but she just wasn't sure. My takeaway was that we weren't believers, and I was content with that.

Until one morning in Mrs. Rosensweig's first-grade class. I was fixating on the tap and scratch of her pointer against the blackboard at the front of our classroom when Martha, who was sitting right next to me, leaned in and whispered a question loudly in my ear.

I was a good girl, determined not to talk in class because Mrs. Rosensweig had a temper. I kept my eyes on the blackboard and on Mrs. Rosensweig, who yelled to keep us quiet, barked at us to line up in height order, and made us march outside for recess.

But Martha was determined to get my attention. She cranked up the whisper volume. "Ellen!" I could feel her breath in my ear, and I couldn't pretend that she wasn't speaking to me anymore.

"Whhhattt?" I mouthed, trying to keep my lips from moving, my eyes straight ahead on Mrs. Rosensweig.

"Do you believe in God?"

I was sure I heard her wrong. My interest was piqued, but I didn't want to draw attention to myself and invite Mrs. Rosensweig's wrath.

"What did you say?"

Martha repeated the question with the emphasis on the

last word. "Do you believe in *God*?" She asked like it was an emergency.

The subject must have come up at Martha's church. Martha knew I was Jewish, and she was probably curious to know what a Jewish girl would say on the subject of God.

So that afternoon in Mrs. Rosensweig's first-grade class, when Martha asked me if I believed in God, a question I had actually been exploring, I replied, "I don't know, but I don't think so."

At this, Martha turned to the girl sitting next to her, cupped a hand over the girl's ear, and speaking loudly enough for me to hear, hissed, "Ellen doesn't believe in God. Pass it on." That girl delivered the same message to the ear of the boy next to her, and a game of whisper-down-the-lane, or telephone, as we used to call it, began.

My jaw went slack. What was she doing? I thought we were friends.

Mrs. Rosensweig heard the whispering, turned from the blackboard, tromped across the classroom in my direction, scowling, and with her long, thin pointer still in her hand, demanded to know what was going on.

I froze.

Martha did not.

"It's Ellen," she boldly offered. "She says she doesn't believe in God."

That's when the sound faded and everything around me went fuzzy, except for Mrs. Rosensweig's face. At the time, before my years at private school, I was in the classroom of a non-parochial, public elementary school where the subject of God and prayer was off limits. A teacher, especially a first-grade teacher, has a number of choices in a moment like that. She could have diverted attention away from the subject and moved back into her lesson. She could have urged me to take the question home to talk with my parents. She could even have turned it into a teaching moment, inquiring about the various religious beliefs in the room. Instead, she stood over me, gesturing madly with her pointer, and began a tirade.

"So you don't believe in God? How could you say such a thing? Where do you think we come from? How do you think you got here this morning? What do you think makes the planes, trains, and cars go?"

As she ranted, all I could feel was the sting of shame in my cheeks and my classmates' eyeballs lasering into me. I had been yelled at before—my father had a temper—but never publicly, and never by a teacher. I remember thinking that her logic made no sense. How did I get to school that day? I walked like I did every morning. And what did God have to do with making the planes, trains, and cars go? I didn't get that at all. The worst of it was her red and puffy face. The longer she spoke, the angrier she got, her eyes bulging with rage.

With one waving hand, this angry, Jewish, God-loving woman had shamed a little girl who dared to say that she wasn't sure if she believed in God. With her other hand, the one gripping a pointer, she seemed to conduct a kind of funeral for big questions, her spittle and sweat extinguishing my sparks of curiosity.

If this is what faith in God looked, sounded, and felt like—punitive, dismissive and illogical—then I wanted no part of it. To my seven-year-old way of thinking, questioning God's existence either brought out a distinct lack of interest or a public tongue-lashing. So I believe that on that day, I buried my curiosity about God, religion, and being Jewish somewhere very deep, and the moment wove itself into the background texture of my childhood memories.

•

After my grandmother left, the house was quiet again. The warm bath pacified and soothed me, and I could still feel ghost-bubbles against my skin. But the spot where my front tooth used to be was still bleeding. I bit down hard on the gauze to keep it steady.

But shortly after, the worries returned.

I thought about burying my face into my pillows, but I was worried about staining them.

I was worried that the bleeding wouldn't stop. What if I fell asleep and my mouth filled with blood? Would I gag and then stop breathing? I worried about Jenny. Caroline. And their mother. I was worried about school. What about my assignments? What would people say? What time was it? Was it too late to call Alysse or Marianne? I couldn't talk with this stupid gauze in my mouth anyway. How would I sleep?

The questions came fast and unrelentingly. I was wide awake most of the night as they ran in circles in my head. I was alone, uncomfortable, and confused. Though my grandmother's bath had been soothing, she was gone now, and no one was beside me telling me I would be okay.

•

In the morning, after a shower, I discovered a bump on my left forefinger, just below my knuckle. I ran two fingers over the hard and pointy spot. Glass. Two slivers. They must have come from the shattered car windows. They were in there, deep. I poked at them with my nail, and my finger bled a little. I considered calling Mom. But I knew how she was about blood and glass, and I didn't want to upset her any more than I already had. I prodded at the bump some more, and finally the pieces came loose. I threw them into the wastebasket in the bathroom and scrounged around for a Band-Aid to cover the wound.

Besides the small hole in my gums, the bandage on my forefinger was the only thing you could see that proved I had been in a car accident.

•

On the way to the dentist, my mother and I stopped at the police station to pick up my book bag. When I looked inside, I found a long, white, bony incisor with a bloody edge. My front tooth had fallen into my blue canvas book bag! Dr. Melman assured us that he could replace it because the tooth had only been out of my mouth for twenty-four hours. I didn't know there was a specific time period for the body to reaccept missing parts. The procedure took most of the day. I sat with my mouth open wide. My jaw was straining, and my butt hurt from sitting. Just a little while longer, he kept saying. I didn't know that a mouth and jaw could get so tired.

When he finished, he placed a small mirror in front of my face. My tooth was back in my mouth, but it was not anything like it had been before. It was put back in with wire and glue. When I ran my tongue over it, it tasted like the inside of a tin can. Dr. Melman ushered Mom into the office, and instead of smiling with relief, she winced. My mouth wasn't bleeding anymore, but the formerly pristine incisor sure wasn't pretty. Mom thanked him and insisted I thank him too.

My tooth was returned to my mouth! If I smiled with my lips held tightly together, it was as if the dentist had erased all visual evidence that I had ever even been in an auto accident.

•

The following Monday I was back at school. "So good to see you, Ellen," Mrs. Bristol, the receptionist at the front desk, said. But no one asked me about the accident. I kept asking my parents how Jenny was but they didn't know, and they didn't pursue it. I begged them to take me to the hospital. My father refused and said that I shouldn't talk about the accident with anyone. I didn't understand why, but I didn't dare challenge him.

I eventually heard—I have no idea from whom—that Jenny had been in a coma for five days after the accident but that she was now awake and alert. She didn't return to school for two and a half months. Those first few weeks I thought about her every day, wondering how she was doing, wanting to go over what happened, to talk to her.

A month or so later, in late May, the seventh-grade parties began. I was invited to Marianne's house. She was one of the popular girls who had been at our private school since kindergarten. Lifers they were called. Lifer social circles were hard to break into, so when Marianne invited me, it felt like I was finally becoming part of the school. I introduced Marianne to my friend Alysse, another new girl whom I had met during the seventh-grade camping trip before school started.

We played Spin the Bottle in Marianne's basement. I kissed a boy for the first time, but it was just a quick peck. Some of the other kids kissed with their mouths open. The next time the bottle neck pointed at me, a boy thrust his tongue deeply in my mouth, and it set off my gag reflex, filling it with the cottony tang of sweet-bitter blood.

I went to more parties. I danced with boys. I watched my classmates pair up and break up and discussed these in great detail with Marianne and Alysse. Then school let out. Summer began, and I went to overnight camp.

But by the time eighth grade started up in the fall, I wasn't thinking about the accident anymore. I felt different. Like a container of feelings I couldn't access or name.

WRESTLING

And Jacob was left alone. And
a man wrestled with him until
the breaking of the day.

—Genesis 32:24

SPRING 1981

BY THE TIME I GOT TO COLLEGE IN THE LATE 1970s, I was a walking, talking, breathing jumble of feelings and sensations I couldn't identify. My family's failure to address the accident felt like a third impact, leaving me reeling. I was rolling along, untethered to any particular future. I studied communications, English, and philosophy but had no idea what I wanted to do with my education or my life.

In the spring of my senior year, I had enough credits to graduate early, gifting me with three months of no classes and parent-paid rent before the dean handed me my bachelor's diploma. I was twenty-one, fresh from a breakup and up for trouble when I heard that the Grateful Dead would be playing a concert at Chicago's Uptown Theatre. So I snagged a ticket.

Before the show, I met up with my friends Katie and Antonio and a few others to eat psychedelic mushrooms mixed with yogurt—a combination I don't recommend—and then we boarded an El train into the city. I was wearing a sky-blue sundress and flowers in my hair, and there was nothing left to do but "smile, smile, smile."

This wasn't my first psychedelic trip, nor my first Dead concert. Drugs and I were well acquainted. I was a weekend weed smoker in high school. Some cocaine too. In college,

I got bolder and experimented with LSD and mushrooms. In all of these scenarios, there was a buddy or boyfriend to babysit me.

This time, however, I was unattached, but because two former boyfriends were in this concert-going group, I needed to stay cool.

We were way up in the nose-bleed seats in this massively large theatre known for its acres of seats, but I was starting to feel claustrophobic. The psychedelics kicked in around the second or third song. Smoke was rising from the main floor, and I needed to get outside. Fast. So I left my seat, and I trotted down the super-wide staircase, stopping to inspect the Baroque carvings on the walls and the ceiling, enamored with the patterns in the carpeting. The music was fading, but already I was feeling better. There was space and so much to see and touch!

Until that moment, my experiences with mind-altering substances had been frolicking affairs, light and lively, littered with forgettable introspections. But in each case, I had taken the drugs in controlled environments. I was now in an uncontrolled one. And I was playing with fire.

I floated out of the theatre and began to skip down Broadway. It wasn't dark yet, but getting there. That's when I saw three lovely young men in a car pull over, park, open the doors, and come toward me. They were smiling and so, of course, I smiled right back. We were all smiling at one another! People were so beautiful. Wasn't the world grand?

There was a language barrier—I don't speak Spanish—but there must have been some kind of conversation. I have zero recollection about what, and since everybody was smiling and getting along so well, sure, I'll get in the car and go anywhere with you! Yes! Yes I will.

One guy opened the rear door and, still smiling, invited me in. Just as I was about to step in, I looked up and saw the desirous expression on his face, and a bell rang in my head, loud and long.

DANGER! THERE'S DANGER AHEAD.

I paused, stepped back and shook my head.

"I can't go with you," I told them. "I'm remembering something I have to do. My friends are over there. I've got to go!"

There was some sort of linguistically challenged discussion. Some attempt to change my mind, but after a few minutes, they let it, and me, go. We were on a major city street dotted with lights, and a commotion would be noticed. There would be no tussle. They got into the car, and I waved to them as they drove off. I was still smiling.

In that moment, I realized I had been incredibly lucky. So incredibly terribly freaking lucky. I had sidestepped serious potential peril.

That's when I began to do that thing I do. The delayed feeling response. My vision began to fuzz. My heart started to pound. I saw a phone booth, and without a moment's more thought, acting on instinct, I made a dash for it as well as a collect call to my parents' house in Philadelphia.

I had been at an out-of-state university for four years and had spent every summer away from home, and this was the first time I had ever called my mother in an emergency.

But in that moment, I wanted my mommy.

I was tripping on a Chicago street when my mother picked up the line and heard the operator say, "Will you accept a collect call from Ellen Blum?"

In the seconds it took for her to accept the charges, I recognized that I was making a terrible mistake. At that time, my mother was great at helping write a resume and cover letter, or problem-solve a relationship. But messy matters of the practical variety, no. I managed to fudge the truth just enough to tell her that I was at a concert, had a bit too much to drink, and was now separated from my friends. The mushrooms would have completely freaked her out.

Her voice was unusually calm. She asked questions like, "How far are you from the venue?" and "You probably need to find one of your friends—I'm sure they will help." And then, "Perhaps you should find a police officer." I think that was the piece of advice that sobered me up a bit. Police? No way! I had just taken illegal drugs. That wasn't going to happen. I thanked her, apologized for worrying her, and assured her I would be fine, and we hung up.

Years later she told me that afterward, she poured a large vodka into a glass, gulped it down, and went right to bed.

But my adventure wasn't over yet. I had lost track of where I was in relation to the theatre. I walked north when I should have walked south. The sky was indigo blue, and it was swirling like van Gogh's brushstrokes. I was alone on a street that didn't feel solid beneath my feet. None of my friends knew I had left the building, so they wouldn't be looking for me, and they were more than likely having adventures of their own. In their heads.

However, mine was on the street. I continued to walk north until I saw a huge metal container in an alley. I could fit in that! So I walked toward it and saw that the top was open. I scrambled in. To be safe, I thought, I should put the top on. I grabbed the hard metal edge, ducked down and let it fall. Boom! I was safe and it was quiet. And I found a curve in the metal so I could see the street and watch for trouble.

But then I felt something squishy under my feet. I looked down. There were smushed McDonald's hamburgers and ketchup-soaked fries. Some other disintegrating food I couldn't identify. And then a terrible rotting smell. That's when I saw the flattened fur and a detached claw! Ugh! A dead rat! Oh, my God, I'm in a freaking dumpster! I've got to get out of here!

I sprang out of that bin and ran without a thought in the other direction. Turns out, the entire time I was outside, I was never more than three blocks away from the theatre. So close but so far away. Like Alice down the rabbit hole that wasn't all that far from her own backyard.

I walked through the doors and approached several stoned theatre staff asking me for my ticket stub. A small tapestry pocketbook hung across my chest, having managed to stay put during my entire journey. My license, apartment key, and a few dollars were in there but no ticket stub.

The stoners smirked and said, "Sorry. You can't come in without a ticket."

"But I was just here! Didn't you see me go out? My friends are here, and I need to find them or I'll never get home!"

On I ranted, but they were having none of it. I was their entertainment for the evening.

"Okay," said one. "You can come back into the theatre if you pick up the trash all over the lobby. Then we'll let you back in."

I paused for a second to see if he was serious. I looked at the other faces, all glaring at me. I was starting to come down from the high and realized there were no other good choices. And so I cleared the entire entrance lobby of the Uptown Theatre of cans and rolling papers and cigarette stubs, and someone handed me a broom and I swept that whole dang lobby.

Thankfully, they made good on their promise. They nodded and pointed to the stairs, and someone said, "Okay, off you go."

I ran so fast up those steps, wiping away tears of humiliation, to the top balcony. When I reached the landing, I heard the opening lines of "It Must Have Been the Roses," and I was smiling again.

Until I reached into my pocket and found my ticket stub.

Back at the seats, I found Katie, tapped her on the shoulder, and she shouted, "Hey there," above the music. "Great show, yeah?" like nothing unusual had happened.

What? Didn't she notice I was gone?

I ran over to Antonio, and he gave me a high five, his face all smiles.

There was one more song, and the show was over. I had missed the whole damn concert with a close call, a tussle with an angel of death. My heart, which had been pumping with a massive amount of adrenaline, began to sink.

This felt familiar. Like I'd been here before. Like I had put myself through a test, pushed against a very strong boundary, just to see if I could. To see if I was invincible.

Only this time, it hadn't been an accident.

STIRRING

If a rock, though extremely hard,
can be hollowed out by water,
how much should it be possible
for the light, which is compared
to water, to change my heart.
I will begin to study it and try to
become a scholar of the light.

—Rabbi Akiva

SPRING 1994

BY THE TIME MY DAUGHTERS WERE SEVEN AND FOUR, I
had become much like my parents. I was uninterested in
Judaism, organized religion, or ritual. I'm not sure if I had
become an atheist or agnostic, but whether God existed or
not wasn't at the top of my mind. My husband, David, grew
up more observantly as a Conservative Jew. At thirteen, he
was bar mitzvahed and was one of the few Jewish kids in
his neighborhood who continued with religious school into
his high school years. We were just starting to think about
looking at synagogues to join when we were invited to a
friend's baby naming, a Jewish ritual in which an infant is
given the Hebrew name that will be used throughout her
lifetime. It's a Jewish baby's formal welcome to her Jewish
community.

When the service began, a woman wearing a beautiful
textured shawl over her shoulders, who looked about six
months pregnant, asked us to gather in a circle. She began to
sing in Hebrew. It took a few minutes, but it finally dawned
on me that she was the rabbi, the first female rabbi I had ever
seen in person.

As she chanted what I later learned was the priestly
blessing recited over children, she began to sway and hum.
I was struck by the beauty and simplicity of her words and

the soul-stirring melody. How the gentle movements of her hands, like tiny conductors, kept us together and engaged, hands that gently touched the baby's head and then led us all in song and celebration.

When she said the word God, *Adonai* in Hebrew, it was her face that captivated me. Her expression was peaceful and relaxed, her expression calm and full of joy. At that moment, Mrs. Rosensweig's red-puffy-angry face was reconjured in my mind's eye. Both the rabbi and Mrs. Rosensweig were Jewish women in authority who believed deeply in the existence of God. But their faces illustrated diametrically opposed expressions of what believing in God could look like. On the rabbi's face, a woman's face, I saw the possibility of a God I could see myself believing in. Some months later we joined that rabbi's synagogue and enrolled my daughters in Sunday religious school. The temple was named Beth Emet, which means "house of truth" in Hebrew, and it felt right.

On the drives to and from school, my oldest daughter, Emily, began to ask questions. Lots of really good questions I couldn't answer.

How old is God?

Where does God live?

Was God Jewish?

Emily was just about the same age I was when I got curious about the subject, and because I remembered how Mrs. Rosensweig had responded to my curiosity, I encouraged my daughter's. Her questions prompted me to facilitate my first spiritual writing workshop. I sat her down at the dining room table and asked her to draw her impressions of God along with words that described what she felt.

"Does it have to be about God?" she asked. "Can I make it about the soul?" I smiled.

Emily was already a voracious reader, incredibly verbal, and not so sure about God, just like her mother at that age. Out of this exercise came her picture book *The Thing That We Call the Soul.*

Your body is for helping the soul out.
Your soul lives in your body.
The soul loves everything it knows of because it is
    kind and gets love back.
Your soul doesn't look like anything—it looks like
    anything you dream of.
As you grow, your soul gets older.
Each soul has a special part which makes it different.
Souls are not religious—they are whatever religion
    you are.
Even animals and plants have souls because they are
    living things.
Your body will die, but your soul won't.
Your soul will never die. It just becomes another thing.
Your soul is a medium-sized ball of God in your body.

A year later, when her younger sister, Jenny, was five, she
wanted to write one too. Jenny penned *A God Book*.

I've never seen God, but I know He has never been
    on television and He is not a relative.
I don't know if God is old, but He is a grownup.
God is a peaceful spirit. He was the first person to die.
God wants to hear laughter.
He sleeps on the clouds.
When you die, you turn into an angel or God turns
    you into a different person.
God likes to make things. He lets the world grow.
During the winter, God makes the summer things.
He makes things for a reason, but I don't know what.
    Maybe because he is lonely.
God never dies.

Children, unwittingly and sometimes prophetically, speak
the truth. It felt like my children sent me into the synagogue
to answer their questions. But I had questions of my own.
And the answers I would find would change everything.

•

The class was called "God." We were discussing the passages from Genesis in which God successfully engages with Abraham over the fate of Sodom and Gomorrah. (Genesis 18:23–26) Abraham asks God if He will deal with the poorly behaved people of Sodom in a just manner. God responds that if He can find fifty righteous people in the city, He will spare everyone.

Some Old Testament or Hebrew Bible scholars called it an argument. Some, a negotiation, a bargaining. But it sounded like a persuasive conversation to me. Before then, never having studied scripture, I had no idea there was any conversing with God. It sounds bizarre to me now, but my younger self's sense of God came from some combination of L. Frank Baum's *The Wonderful Wizard of Oz* and Charlton Heston's portrayal of Moses in *The Ten Commandments*. To me, God was a fear-inducing, cartoonish presence who demanded and commanded. And if one dared to argue, one would be smote.

I wasn't aware of it at the time, but now that I think of it, the image was very similar to the fear I had about angering my father. Angering him would lead to yelling or discipline of some kind, much like a punitive version of God that discouraged argument or discussion.

Judaism is, by its very nature, an ongoing conversation. There are endless commentaries on every sentence of Torah, the five books of the Hebrew Bible. The commentaries have commentaries. One page of Talmud, the primary source of Jewish laws, contains numerous rabbinic perspectives. Some might even say Judaism is a long series of arguments that sound like everyone is talking over one another, like my husband's family's seders. That the Torah contained stories of human beings who spoke directly and even argued with God and stayed alive was a game changer.

In addition to the arguments, there are contradictions and paradoxes. You can find it in the language itself. Many

Hebrew words contain a thing as well as its opposite. The Hebrew word for "stranger," for example, comes from the word "recognition." The word for sin can also be used to suggest purification. Judaism allows for at least two truths, two ways to look at a thing, and both may be correct. There isn't just black or white, right or wrong. And this felt like something I could call home.

•

Six years later, I had taken enough courses to prepare for an adult bat mitzvah: God; Basic Judaism; Hebrew I, II, and III; Cantillation; Jewish History; Exploring Genesis; Exploring Exodus. I loved Jewish adult education. I couldn't get enough of it. Judaism is word-centric. Book honoring. Story driven. Discussion heavy. Philosophical and morality based. I rediscovered my seven-year-old curiosity about God that hadn't ever left; it was just buried under shame and fear. My children's curiosity was like the *ner tamid* ("the eternal light"): a small, glowing light that hangs in every synagogue and never goes out.

I took my Jewish studies further. I joined a Torah study group, and the rabbi pointed out that God's first words—Let there be light—brought the universe into creation. Spoken words manifested big things.

It was only after God blew "the breath of life" into Adam's nostrils, whom God created from the dust of the earth, that Adam became a living being. The body and the soul in Judaism are understood as separate but interconnected partners in human beings. The body is a tool God provides us to be used to do sacred work in the world. The soul is a guest in the body, and taking care of the soul is considered a commandment. In Hebrew, *neshama* means both breath and soul. It made me wonder about my breath after the truck hit our car. I was suffocated when my mouth was pushed into the seatback. Was there a release or did I hold my breath? And what did this mean for my soul?

•

At thirty-nine, I was one of ten adult women who were bat mitzvahed, and I threw myself a party. I wanted to do it, in part, for my daughters, to show them that I wouldn't ask them to do anything I hadn't done myself. But mostly I wanted to earn my place in the Jewish community.

A few months after the ceremony, the director of education asked if I would be interested in teaching religious school. I was honored to be asked, but I had never, not for a second, thought of teaching. I had been an average student in high school and college. School had never been my thing. So I thanked her and took a pass.

A year later, she asked me again.

"I have an opening for a fifth-grade religious school teacher," she said. "Sunday mornings. The curriculum covers God, Israel, and *tzedakah*, the doing of good deeds. You'd be mentored." My daughters were in high school and middle school and busy with activities and social lives, and my freelance assignments were starting to lag.

"There's bagels and coffee. And you'd be paid."

She had my attention.

I picked the right year to say yes. The temple had received a grant to provide teacher education. It meant staying later on Sundays for intensive teacher training along with lunch every Sunday over a two-year period. We studied pedagogy and the art of how we learn. The level of discussion and deeper dive into Jewish texts was so profoundly moving that I briefly considered applying to rabbinical school. I was stunned to discover how much I loved teaching. It combined so many things I enjoyed: creativity, writing, discussion, improvisation, song, art, reading. I was ignited by the energy and enthusiasm of ten- and eleven-year-olds, and the school encouraged us as teachers to stir their questions, even the hardest ones.

•

Keeping the attention of thirteen fifth-graders focused on God, Israel, and *tzedakah* on a Sunday morning from 9:30 to noon was incredibly challenging. When it was time to get into the God unit, I knew it was going to be dicey. How does one teach God to an eleven-year-old? So much of a child's belief system comes from what they are picking up at home. In addition, my congregation was full of interfaith families, so the language we used to talk about God had to be sensitive. And I still wasn't entirely sure about my own faith as I continued to struggle with doubt. How does one teach around these emotional and spiritual minefields?

There was one student, Ben, whose attention I had trouble catching all year. He spent most of the time doodling on a piece of paper, rarely looking up or engaging with his classmates. I was concerned enough to inquire about him. He struck me as depressed. I learned that his parents were in the midst of a divorce, and my directive was not to worry, but to keep an eye on him.

One Sunday in late spring, I offered the students a notebook, a pencil, and a writing prompt. We went outside to the playground, and I asked them to look around for signs of God. I gave them ten minutes to search followed by ten minutes to write. Delighted to be outside in the sunshine, the students got to it. Except for Ben. He sat on the edge of the sandbox, refusing to look around or do anything more than stare down at his notebook.

I approached him.

"Nothing striking your eye, Ben?"

"Nope."

"Hmmm . . . What about those birds flying overhead? The bugs over here in the sand? Those daffodils about to bloom?"

"Well, those aren't signs of God."

"Why do you say that?"

"Well, because there is no God."

I took a deep breath, remembering to encourage questions. I carefully selected my words.

"I'd be curious to hear how you know that."

"I just know."

"How do you know?"

"Because I don't see God. Or feel God."

At that, Ben looked up for the first time. I met his steady gaze. He wasn't going to budge on this without a scene. And I didn't want to turn this into a scene because I'll never forget the scene Mrs. Rosensweig made with her pointer and her rant.

As an adult, my own beliefs about God were still under construction. I was the mother of a daughter who was questioning the existence of God. I was also a religious-school teacher whose job it was to encourage my students to think about God. What I said could stick with him forever.

All I could think to do in that moment was answer him the way I wished Mrs. Rosensweig has answered me.

"Okay, Ben. I'm glad you shared that with me. And I appreciate your honesty."

I think about Ben from time to time. Wherever it was that he landed on his journey toward or away or somewhere in the middle with God, I hope he feels he came to it without any detours caused by his religious school teachers getting in the way.

RETURNING

You grow, in part, by returning.

—David Ebenbach

SPRING 2006

I WAS IN MY OFFICE CLOSET, AGAIN, RUSTLING THROUGH the binders of my newspaper columns when I came upon the plastic boxes containing my journals. It had been almost a decade since my reunion conversation with Jenny, and I still hadn't found a single mention of the accident.

A few weeks after my return from that reunion, Jenny and I spoke by phone. I remember it as a pleasant exchange, mostly a confirmation of the facts we had already discussed. Our call gave me the chance to ask a few more questions about what she remembered, and she provided an eerily detailed account of the seconds before the impact, where the car was in relation to the truck and where each of us was on the inside. I was amazed at her precision, despite the coma that followed. But I couldn't bring myself to ask what I most wanted to know. What happened to us? I didn't know if something ominous had transpired between our parents or if something I said could have changed everything. I wanted to know, but my fear of what it was or of upsetting her exceeded my desire for knowledge. So I shoved my curiosity aside. Again.

Our conversation ended on a friendly note, but in the days and weeks after, I felt like the ground beneath me had shifted. My storyline was shaky. Memory, unreliable.

It was becoming physical. The entire area around my mouth hurt. It was mostly my jaw, at times my teeth, and sometimes even down into my neck. I can see the constriction in photographs taken of me then. I was getting headaches from the pressure of my clenched teeth in spite of the mouth guard that I wore every night. I suspected there was a connection between the accident and my increasing pain, and I thought that if some key detail could be revealed about the nature, angle, and force of the impact, perhaps it would help illuminate something.

I shared this thought with Marianne over the phone one afternoon during one of our many long calls.

"I know you think there's something to find," she said, gently, a "but" clearly to follow. "But I'm not getting why you are so obsessed. It was way worse for Jenny and her sister and mom."

It was beyond awful for them. I knew that. I had been trying to imagine how life had been for Jenny and Caroline right after the accident. What it must have felt like for Jenny to have to relearn how to walk and talk. And then, some years later, to lose her mother! I just lost a few days of school, some blood, and a front tooth. It was only the slightest deviation for me. But Jenny's and Caroline's entire lives changed. Knowing this made me feel worse for my moping and for all of those blanks. But there was something more, I just knew it, felt it, something I desperately needed to discover.

On the phone with Alysse, who before working toward her landscaping degree had counseled troubled teens, questioned my motives. "What are you looking for? What do you think you will find that will make you feel better?"

"I really don't know. But I certainly don't feel good about it all now."

Even David, who mostly kept his opinions to himself unless I pushed, reminded me how lucky I had been. "There's no doubt it was a terrible accident, E. You were young and it was scary. But you were very lucky."

My posse was losing patience with me. I, too, was tiring from carrying the heavy weight of this mission. I wanted nothing more than to forget the whole thing. I told myself that I experienced a very close call, a brush with death, and was incredibly fortunate to come out the other side with some simple dental work. There was nothing more to do. I really tried to put it out of my mind.

But I felt stalked, haunted. I noticed it especially in a car. My daughters were learning to drive, and it didn't take long for all of us to recognize that I wasn't the parent for that job. Even in the back seat, with David calmly providing step-by-step instructions, my jaw would lock up. I was anxious. Overly alert. Every turn, every ragged stop, every hesitation a reminder of how close we are, every minute of the day, to the possibility of everything changing in an instant.

•

It was one of those rare, glorious spring-is-finally-here Saturdays in Chicago, and David took the girls out on their bikes, which was significant for more than weather-related reasons. David was just a year out from a health scare that almost took him from us. Five blockages in the arteries around his heart. Quintuple bypass surgery. At forty-seven.

A cycling friend had identified the early symptoms. David had been lagging behind his usual pace on the road. I'll never forget the morning after he returned home from a bike ride one winter night. He woke as cold to the touch as he was when he fell into bed. David was stubborn about going to a doctor. He was stubborn about a lot of things, but his bike buddies kept at him. Hank finally emailed me to report his concern. After I printed the email and left it on his pillow, David acquiesced, finally making the medical appointment that led to his diagnosis.

It took a small village to get David to see the doctor and to help pull us both through. That village included David's biking friends who first saw his slowed pace while riding. The endocrinologist who discovered his type 2 diabetes. The cardiologist who found the blockages. Friends and neighbors who came to the hospital in the days before and after his surgery. Out-of-state friends who called and emailed and sent gifts after he returned home.

Through that whole ordeal, it occurred to me that I never had seen my parents visit people who were sick or drop off food or flowers or send cards. I don't ever recall going to Jenny's house to see her after the accident. I remember asking to go, but I also remember my parents' rebuffs.

The message I got was that being sick or injured was a private thing. Being unwell was about staying in bed, remaining behind closed doors. People should see you at your best—even in photographs. My mother only kept the pictures in which my brother and I were dressed up like little dolls. When people come over, they should be entertained. One didn't go to people's houses when they weren't well, even to drop off a gift. But I discovered that when David was sick, it was soothing to have people understand that we had been through something difficult, acknowledge our pain, and want to make us feel better. Like my Grandma Jane had done for me with that bath. Her love and attention were everything to me that evening after the crash.

Jews go to the sick and injured. We sit with them. The Talmud says that a visit from one person takes away one-sixtieth of a person's pain.

David was back at work in his law office in three weeks and back on his bike in six.

Excellent medical care and good health insurance were a huge part, but that small village may have been just as important. I know it helped his healing. David knows it too.

•

It was spring in Chicago and I was pining for Philadelphia. I had been on the East Coast fairly regularly in the nine years since the reunion, usually taking my daughters to the New Jersey shore in summer to visit my father and Fran, who had a house there, or to see my mother, who was living in Manayunk with her boyfriend. I managed to get to Philadelphia once or twice a year. Keeping my daughters connected to my side of the family, all of whom lived out of town, felt worth the effort, but since they had become freshmen in college and high school, schedules were harder, almost impossible, to align.

The longing was more like an itch that I couldn't scratch until I went. I love Chicago, but spring never feels like spring to me in the Midwest. Winter doesn't lose its grip until the end of May or early June. I hankered to see Alysse and Marianne, with whom I managed to keep up by phone but whose live company I missed.

It could have been my daughter's driving lessons. Maybe the conversations with Alysse and Marianne. Or the season. But an idea began to materialize.

What if I interviewed Jenny and Caroline about how the accident impacted our lives? I could explore how our shared trauma revealed itself across our lifetime. How differently it felt for each woman. To find out what it was like for Jenny and Caroline. To figure out what happened to my friendship with Jenny and what kept us from talking about the accident. The effort could pull together the threads, identify the missing parts, help me, and perhaps each of us, heal. The idea elated me. I knew how to do this. This was something I could do.

I reached out to Caroline first, thinking that if she was in, this might make Jenny feel more comfortable. I had the sense that Jenny would be open to talking about the facts, but I wasn't sure she would be up for discussing what happened after. I located Caroline's email address from the school alumni office, reached out, and she emailed back the following day.

"It may be that our memories are somewhat asynchronous," she wrote. "It sounds like an interesting project for you, but I regret that I am not that interested in participating."

This was going to be more difficult than I thought.

While it was undoubtedly a distressing experience for you, it was an event that changed and actually destroyed my immediate family. . . . I have spent a life wondering what my family would have been like if that Volkswagen and truck hadn't met that afternoon when I was in ninth grade, thinking about a solo I had just been given in *Trial by Jury* as we took you home. . . . I don't know that there is any great lesson to be learned.

Then she added:

In an interesting side note, a move that I understand now, but didn't then—your parents sued my mother for the injuries you sustained. I saw my mother's face as she came back from the front door, in her wheelchair, distressed and confused, as the process server left the papers. I assume that it was all dealt with by insurance, but at the time I was totally and completely outraged and offended at what I viewed as a horribly hurtful thing given the comparatively minor injuries and consequences you sustained. I swore then that I would become a defense lawyer. I did. An interesting outcome. I appreciate the contact, completely understand it, and am by no means upset or offended. Kind regards, Caroline.

A lawsuit! Not only did my parents not reach out with kindness to Jenny's family, it appears they did quite the opposite. It was the first I had heard of this. I had no idea. This was mortifying! I was starting to understand the cautious expression I saw on Jenny's face at the reunion.

I was compelled to respond. I needed Caroline to know that there was so much I didn't know. I emailed saying how sorry I was that she felt this way. That I didn't know about the lawsuit, but I did know how lucky I was, injury-wise. That I had been making connections between the accident and some physical issues. That I was starting to believe my jaw pain was not so much a result of the accident but of how it was handled afterward, that there had been a successful silencing. I told her about the absence of information about the accident in my diaries and about the little figurine without a mouth. I thanked her for providing me with some background and signed it "With warm regards."

She surprised me with this response:

> I absolutely agree with you that talking about things at the time would have been much better! It just "wasn't done"—and I think all of us would have benefited from being able to address what we were feeling. I know we were all being "protected" but I am not sure from what. Today, once the immediate physical issues were addressed, counseling would be next on the list! I am distressed to learn the extent of the issues that you have had over the years. It was unfair of me to assume that it was not something that had major long-term effects.... I have no idea why this "cone of silence" came down.... I have often thought about how small moments can cause huge changes. One minute you're driving home from school with your mom, and the next your whole world is turned completely upside down and inside out. So for all that I said I didn't want to participate, here I am giving you even more information. I hope it is helpful to you—even if it is just context. Best of luck to you! Caroline.

Her words were heartbreaking to read. It wasn't just me who was silenced. We were all silenced. "Protected," as Caroline put it. But from what? If only we could have shared this with one another back then. How differently this might have played out for each of us.

Caroline was out for reasons I understood. She had been through enough and had a right to her privacy.

But I wasn't ready to give up just yet. I was determined to get Jenny on board. It was a side of myself that I didn't recognize. It felt like compulsion. To get the story. Like it was an emergency.

I emailed Jenny, and she responded that same day:

The accident was life-altering for all of my family, so going through everything again would be very difficult. I cannot contribute because it would definitely mean going into some tough times; "powerful and emotional," as you said in your letter. If you have any questions about the actual accident, I can probably answer them for you. Don't know why, but I remember just about all of it—date, time, how the accident happened. Best to you and your family.

It was another rejection. Thoughtfully and graciously given, but a rejection nonetheless. A reminder to me of how big this was and how successfully I—we?—had pushed it aside.

I fell back into what was becoming a familiar, welcoming, numbing silence.

•

That same spring I was on my way to pick my daughter Jenny up from soccer practice that had been canceled due to threat of rain. A thick fog hung in the air. About eight blocks from my house, I came to a full stop at an intersection, leaned to the passenger seat to take a bite of a turkey sandwich I'd grabbed before I left the house. I had been lost in a writing assignment and hadn't eaten anything since breakfast. I put the remains of it back on the passenger seat, quickly looked both ways, and turned left into the intersection. The next thing I knew, my car, which had been facing north, was now facing west, having landed with an abrupt halt on the front lawn of a house across the street, and I was struggling for breath.

Except for the pressure on my chest from a working seatbelt, I was physically fine. Except for his mournful "fuckohfuckohfuck" over the completely crushed front end of his car, the twenty-something with whom I collided was okay too. Our cars, however, were totaled. Three police officers arrived swiftly on the scene, as did an immense tow truck, medics from a nearby hospital, and my dear friend and neighbor Sean.

The police officers asked how I was doing. Surveying the scene, the tow truck driver and the medics spoke gently and respectfully, telling me that the young man and I were very lucky.

We were lucky, he and I. That's three times lucky for me. Twice in a car. Once before getting in one.

It was foreign and familiar at the same time, but this time, I was bathed in a bubble of care. Sean was quick with a hug, and after seeing that I was okay for the moment, began to take cell phone pictures for the insurance company. After my car was towed, she escorted me to her car, delivered me safely home, and put the kettle on.

My daughter found a ride home with someone else's mother, though I worried about that ride home until she arrived at the door, and then she sat down at the dining room table beside me, stroking my back protectively while she poured me a cup of tea. I called David and he left work right away. When he arrived home, he gave me a big hug and encouraged me to write down what I remembered. He was steady in a crisis, always thinking like a lawyer, and got on the phone with the insurance company.

Later I recognized that this second accident had been a "do over."

I was heading north, just as I was in 1972. After the collision, I ended up facing west. According to rabbinic literature, the divine presence, the *shekinah*, can be found in the westward directions.

The collision occurred at the same time of year—spring—and roughly the same time of day, thirty-four years later. I was grown now, the driver instead of a passenger, but this time we were talking about it, acknowledging what could have happened and feeling incredibly grateful for what hadn't.

I began to think of it as a non-accidental healing.

Jenny and Caroline may have opted out of this story that we shared. But I was starting to understand that there was a story within this story that was, indeed, uniquely mine.

•

In the weeks after the accident, which was so eerily like the one decades before, I found myself reflecting on the mystery of things. Was this second accident just another close call? Another lucky break? Or might it be an offering from the universe, or God, for a second chance to heal? Something inside told me that it was more than just coincidence or luck. I was beginning to feel more comfortable calling this an act of God, an aspect of divine presence. It was around this time that I decided to take a class on Jewish mysticism—Kabbalah—at a local synagogue. I learned about the ten *sefirot*—the ten attributes, manifestations, or emanations of God. I read Daniel Matt, an expert on the Zohar, the mystical Jewish text, who wrote that if God spoke the world into being with the words "Let there be light," then the divine language is energy. Elemental particles of energy, the laws of nature, are God's grammar, how God thinks and reveals Godself to human beings. That's when I first learned about the light, the brokenness, and the call to repair.

According to Kabbalah, as the Infinite began to unfold, a ray of light was channeled into that void through vessels. Everything went smoothly at first. But some of the vessels were not translucent enough. They couldn't withstand the power of the light and they shattered. Most of the light then returned to its Infinite source, to the mother's womb.

But the rest fell as sparks along with broken shards of the shattered vessels. And those sparks were eventually trapped in the material world. Our task, according to Kabbalah, is to liberate these sparks of light, to restore them to God by raising the sparks, by living ethically and spiritually. This is how we restore the light, how we repair and mend the cosmos.

These ideas stimulated me in a deep way. I was feeling flickers of what I think was a spiritual awakening. But emotionally, I was floundering. Distracted. Uneven-tempered. My patience more thin than usual with David and the girls. My usual comfort mechanisms—a walk, a yoga class, a call with Alysse or Marianne, writing in my journal or drinking a glass of wine, even therapy and St. John's wort—weren't working. So I made flight reservations for Philadelphia. I was getting familiar with this compulsive side of myself and something was making me trust it.

I was going solo, just like I did for my twentieth reunion and several other trips to Philadelphia to see family and friends. David rearranged his schedule to be the primary parent for the girls for a few days, for which I was grateful. They actually loved it when I went out of town so they could be alone with their dad for a change of pace. But I sensed that privately he was shaking his head, wondering what I thought I would find.

I told everyone I was going to see Alysse, Marianne, and the azaleas that bloom psychedelically in lush red, purple, and pink flower fireworks every Philadelphia spring. But I was really going with a shovel and a pail to finish off this psychospiritual-archeological dig.

I was staying at Alysse's because Marianne has two cats, and in recent years, I had become allergic. Alysse's front and back yard overflowed with azaleas bushes. Alysse, Marianne, and I had plans for dinner Friday night.

It had been a dreadful few years for all of us. I was still recovering from the surprise of David's heart surgery, but the last few years had been especially challenging for

Alysse and Marianne. Two years before, Alysse had been working on a landscaping project when she was struck with excruciating back pain. Over the course of several days, the pain worsened. By the time she got to the hospital, she learned she had suffered an arterial venous malformation, a stroke in her spine. She had become paralyzed from the waist down. It was a shock on so many levels. She was now navigating life from a wheelchair, but Alysse was astonishing me with how well she had been faring since the stroke. She drove a big van with hand controls that allowed her to pick up her sons, do errands, and get to her work sites, and she insisted on living life as close to the way in which she had before.

That same year Marianne had lost her mother to Parkinson's disease. Six months later, her father died from complications of lung cancer. Just a month before my visit, her husband had suffered from heart failure. She had been handling all of it heroically while simultaneously holding things together for her husband and daughter. I was in awe, my heart breaking for both of them, especially because I lived so far away, unable to do for them what I had experienced when David was sick. I just wanted to be able to drop off dinner or pick up a child to lend any kind of real hand beyond supportive calls and emails.

My reason to be in Philadelphia paled profoundly by comparison. We were in our late forties. Alysse and Marianne were facing physical disability, severe illness, and death. I, however, was in town to explore an accident in which I had merely lost a tooth. They wished me well, and I suspected that like David, they were weary of this. Besides, they had plenty on their own plates right now.

It plagued me that I couldn't articulate why I felt so unresolved about this chapter of my life. I worried that if I couldn't explain it to Alysse and Marianne, if they were right that I was making a big deal out of nothing, then what did that make me? "Too sensitive?" as my father often said of me. David, from time to time, had said so too. I understand that being sensitive is part of being a creative person, a writer. But could you be overly sensitive? I wanted to think of myself as strong, like the women I kept close. Like the women I wanted my daughters to become.

But I had traveled all this way, so I borrowed my mother's Honda Civic and returned to the intersection of Carpenter and McCallum. Decades had passed since I had last been to this part of Philadelphia. I parked and stood in the middle of the street, the site of the initial crash. Then I crossed and positioned myself where I imagined the second impact took place. I took photographs. Cars came and went at infrequent intervals; it wasn't a very busy intersection. I was there maybe twenty minutes, waiting to feel something. But I felt nothing. Standing in the intersection, no one around, I recognized I was sensationless. How was that possible? Wasn't I supposed to be so sensitive?

I was desperately hoping that at least one of the conversations I had scheduled with my parents would help shake this numbness loose. I wanted to feel something about the accident. Something true. Something mine.

•

I met my mother at a deli near Alysse's house. At seventy she was still working full time as a career counselor. She had been living with Roy for more than twenty years. Like my father in his marriage to Fran, she was happy and settled in her relationship.

My mother looked great. Her skin was dewy, there was light in her hazel eyes, and whoever was coloring her dark brown hair into this shade of blonde was doing a great job; her hair had actual bounce. Weekly yoga classes and acupuncture may have been helping her look ten years younger than she was, or maybe it was because Roy cooked vegetarian meals every night. She was full of energy and curiosity, still the single biggest supporter of my career, even before I had one, insisting that I write my resume while I was babysitting and working summer retail jobs in high school. Because she suspected I would be writing about our conversation—writing being my vocation, vocation being her thing—she was on board.

Over her half of a six-inch-high corned beef sandwich on rye with Russian dressing and cole slaw—I got one every time I returned to Philly, unless I was anywhere near a cheese steak or soft pretzel stand—I interviewed my mother. She knew I wanted to talk about the accident even though she had already told me she didn't remember much. But by talking about it together, face to face, I told her, there was a good chance she would remember more than she thought she did. I certainly had seen it happen during my journalistic interviews.

She delicately picked up her half-sandwich and was looking for the right spot to take the first bite. My stomach was in knots, so I was saving mine for after our conversation.

"I remember the call from the police, or was it the hospital? I'm not sure. But it was terrifying to get the call, really terrifying."

"Did you ever see the car or the truck afterward?"

"No, honey . . . " She was becoming preoccupied with her sandwich. She was an empowered professional woman who placed a high value on tidiness, but she still, quite literally, couldn't stand a mess. "How ever do you eat this thing?"

After she finished chewing, which felt like five long minutes, she said, "I didn't see it, but I remember the relief I felt when I found out you were okay and I could take you home. There was just a lot of blood coming from your tooth socket. I remember that."

"But what about after, Mom? What happened after?" I was trying to keep my voice calm, trying to be empathetic to the reality of memory. She had lived seven decades, but I was having trouble accepting how much my mother forgot. Or shoved aside. Or simply didn't want to face. But I pulled myself together. Like me, she was sensitive, and if she picked up that I was upset, she'd get upset, too, and my effort to shake loose some new detail would be lost.

We had yet to make eye contact as she was completely distracted by her four-layer sandwich. She put it down and removed the inner bread layers to make it thinner. She took a dull knife from the table and began to carefully slice it into four squares.

"Mom?"

"Yes?" she said, lost in her sandwich surgery.

"After. We were talking about after."

"All I remember is taking you to the dentist the next day. We went back for months and months after that. Your lost tooth complicated your braces, and so we had endless visits to the dentist and orthodontist. Your father spoke to the lawyer and handled the suit."

I definitely remembered those dentist and orthodontist visits. It felt like I spent most of my adolescence in those offices. But I wanted to know more about the legal issue.

"That was your dad's thing, honey. I stayed out of it," she said, our eyes finally meeting for the first time since we had sat down in the booth.

"The lawyer counseled him not to talk about the accident because it could get in the way of the suit. He didn't want any of us talking to anyone else about it, either."

"But what could I, or any of us, possibly have said to mess it up?"

Eyes back on her sandwich, my mother said, "I really don't know."

I considered pressing her, but decided against it. Because I believed her. She really didn't know. That time long ago was a dried-up mix of worry, relief, and marital distress that ultimately led to a new relationship and a new life for her.

I had rustled up enough dust for the time being.

•

My conversation with my father was scheduled for the following day, Sunday, the only day he could meet given his schedule. It was also my last day in Philadelphia, and I only had an hour before I needed to leave for the airport. At the appointed time, I showed up at his house, the same one where I had discovered the figurine nearly a decade before.

My father was in his mid-seventies now, still a few years from retirement. I was nervous. I wasn't sure how this conversation would go. When I scheduled this visit, I told him that I wanted to talk about the accident. I just wanted information. But I worried that he would feel attacked. This conversation was going to challenge him.

We were sitting on iron chairs on his flagstone patio by the goldfish pond. It was April and still cool by the tall trees on this side of Fairmont Park. I heard the gurgling of the water pump for the pond and the tweeting of birds. There wasn't much time after pleasantries and chitchat before I had to catch a cab to the airport.

My father's nose was dripping; a cold. After several rejected offers of iced tea and reminders for him to take the cold tablets she slipped into his hand, which he finally swallowed without water, Fran left to run some errands, and I got right to it.

"So, Dad. What do you remember about the day of the accident?"

He cleared his throat and then released a loud, breathy sigh and a phlegm-clearing grunt. He was taking his time, noticeably uncomfortable, but I couldn't tell if it was the cold or the content of our conversation.

"Your mother called me at the office to tell me you'd been in a car accident," he said. "When I got home, you seemed fine except for your tooth—it was your tooth, right?"

"Yes. My front left tooth."

"I remember now. I called the lawyer right away."

"Why did we need a lawyer?"

"There were bills to pay. Dental and orthodontic procedures, as I recall. We sued and got enough to cover the medical costs."

"Tell me about the suit."

"We filed a suit but it took a while for the money to come through."

"Was it against the trucking company or the family?"

"Don't remember."

Those two words. They exasperated me when my mother said them, but hearing my father repeat them heightened my frustration. I knew that memory was fluid, especially for a seventy-something man. But "don't remember" felt like code for "I don't want to remember."

It felt like a door shutting.

"You can't recall any other details, Dad?"

My father shook his head. His eyes were defocusing. I felt he was losing interest in the conversation.

"Did you ever talk to the police?"

"Don't recall." Then one eyelid began to droop.

"Or Jenny's mother or father?"

He released a huge yawn. And then, "What did you say?"

"Do you remember seeing the accident site or a photograph?"

"No."

"Did we visit Jenny in the hospital or at home?"

"The lawyer didn't want us to talk with the family. I didn't know them. It was a legal matter."

"I don't get that, Dad. How was talking about it going to impact anything?"

He shrugged. His other lid began to sink.

I sighed.

"Did we reach out at all? A card or flowers?"

One of his eyes was now completely closed.

"Dad? Are you with me?"

His hand went limp and hung from the arm of his chair.

My father often fell asleep in front of the television, but never had I witnessed it during a conversation. This was the first and only time I had ever gone to such efforts to gather information that only he could provide.

Could the cold tablets have taken effect that fast?

"Huh?" he said, his left lid up, eye dazed, and the other shut. "What'd you say?"

I was frustrated. My all-business guard, down. I had lost my patience.

"Nothing else comes to mind?"

"Nothing. Sorry." At this, both his eyes closed. I swear I heard a slam.

•

On my way back to Chicago, I pulled back the cardboard accordion window shade, leaned my cheek into the small, white pillow and stared blankly into the clouds. My father fell asleep in the middle of a conversation that I had come so far to have. I had worked hard to prepare for this trip; I had hoped for something concrete, tangible. But there were no more questions left to ask, no more documents to scour, no more notes to scribble. I had been through the ruins, dug up what there was to find, and it was all dry gravel and sand. I prepared for the heavy crush of disappointment, but it didn't come.

I found myself returning to a familiar place, back to numb.

SPEAKING

I don't speak because I have the power to speak; I speak because I don't have the power to remain silent.

—Rabbi A. Y. Kook

SPRING 2012

I WAS IN COLORADO COMBINING A VISIT TO SEE Marianne, who had just moved to Denver with her husband, with my father's seventy-eighth birthday celebration in Aspen. He and Fran spend the summer months there to be near Fran's children and grandkids.

Marianne was acclimating to the West after a lifetime on the East Coast, a huge adjustment. I thought it would be fun to introduce her to Fran's daughter-in-law who had worked as an interior designer and had an artistic eye. She and Marianne shared exquisite taste, and I thought they might click. Perhaps she could recommend some galleries that might be interested in selling Marianne's paintings or introduce her to the Aspen arts community. Marianne generously offered to drive me the four hours from Denver to Aspen. She planned to stay the night with me and head back to Denver the following day.

I set up a coffee date for five of us: Marianne, Fran, Fran's daughter, daughter-in-law, and me. Everyone was on board.

The day before Marianne and I were scheduled to leave Denver for Aspen, I called Dad to confirm directions and timing. We were winding down, and just as I was about to hang up, he asked, "What's this about a coffee you arranged?"

"It's coffee, Dad. I thought it would be nice to get everyone together."

"Hmmm . . . " His voice had an accusing edge. "Well, you know I'm on to you."

I was used to this line of teasing, but I didn't like the tone in his voice.

"What do you mean, 'on to me'?"

"I know what you're trying to do."

"What are you talking about?"

"It's clear what you're doing."

"Dad, what exactly are you suggesting?"

"You are trying to sell Marianne's paintings."

Anger was beginning to stir, but I took a breath and felt strangely grounded too.

Marianne's paintings are spectacular. Given the chance or interest, I'll bring out my phone and show anyone her website. I had even produced events to help promote them. But what he was suggesting hadn't even crossed my mind.

"No, Dad," I said calmly. "That was never my intent. But frankly, if anyone wanted to look at Marianne's work and was interested enough to purchase a painting, then that would be great. What would be wrong with that?"

It was quiet on his end.

My father had accused me of many things in my life that I wasn't actually doing. Having sex with a boyfriend before I was actually having it. Taking money from Mom's purse when I didn't. Being overly sensitive. Selfish. But this. This was beyond any of those.

He was suggesting that my ride from Denver to Aspen to attend his birthday party was a scheme to get a painting sold for a friend? Really?

It occurred to me that this was something he might think to do. If it was my plan, I would be transparent about it. But clandestine operations weren't my modus operandi.

An incredibly intense feeling of rage, a familiar one, welled up. Normally, I would just listen and go numb. But this time, I heard myself say, "Dad, I don't know where this is coming from, but I can't listen to this anymore. This accusation is insulting, and I am going to hang up now."

I had never said that to my father before. I had never said it to anyone before.

"No, no, don't hang up," he implored. "Let me explain."

I hesitated, but curiosity won out.

He explained that because Fran's children had done well in business, he didn't want his side of the family to appear financially obsequious in any way. A deep sadness washed over me. My father's agenda was his own. He was focused on financials over family.

I had heard enough. I was livid. I had never felt that much anger before.

I told him I wouldn't be attending his birthday party, and I hung up the phone, on my father, for the first time in my life.

Seconds after the words left my mouth, my knees buckled and I collapsed onto the sidewalk in deep, heaving sobs. Marianne held me as I pulsated under a lamplight on a Denver street corner for what felt like a really long time.

That night was a turning point. I drew a line, made by my own tears on the street. My response wasn't preplanned or premeditated.

No, I will not be accused of something I did not do.

No, I will not be dismissed.

No, my intentions were not about self-interest.

Some hours later, after I had let it all out, some calm returned, and we made the decision to salvage the next several days by heading to Marianne's friend's condominium an hour away. We packed up and left swiftly to spend the next forty-eight hours cooking, hiking, and watching back-to-back seasons of *Mad Men* on Netflix.

In between our walks in the mountains, when there was cell service, texts from my brother, who was already in Aspen for the festivities, piled in, begging me to reconsider. He wrote that Dad had been called out by the rest of the family and was feeling bad and desperately wanted me to come. Later, my father texted that he would send a car for me. He would meet me in Vail and drive us back to Aspen.

I was starting to waffle just a little. I sensed remorse. Or maybe I wanted his remorse. I wasn't entirely sure which was true. Not showing up at his birthday party was a big deal. I had never traveled out of state for his birthday and then not shown up. Everyone knew this. They knew he must have done something to push his daughter to make that choice.

What I did know, however, was that I had made a huge impression by my absence. I had made myself visible by not showing up, by making myself invisible.

I began to reconsider. He was in his seventies. Who knew how much time was left for our limited get-togethers? I was relenting. Marianne was dubious. She may have been right, but something larger called. I decided to go for one day and one night.

The following morning, I pulled Marianne close, thanked her and apologized, and a stranger drove me the hour to Vail in a black SUV. At our rendezvous point, my father pulled up in a gray SUV, and I got into the front seat. His face was grim. There was a long silence, and then he said, "I made a terrible error in judgment." It wasn't an actual apology, but it was the closest I was going to get to one. He sounded sorry. Regretful. I listened to him for about ten minutes, and it felt good to hear him acknowledge how painful this had been for me. It was the first time in fifty-three years that he was acknowledging my feelings. It was returning some balance, but not enough to keep me from having my say.

"Okay, Dad. I've heard you. I have a few things to say. Will you hear me out?"

He nodded. I saw his expression shift as he kept his eyes looking straight ahead on the winding Colorado switchbacks. Perhaps he had hoped that would be the end of it. But it was incredibly rare for me to be alone with my father—it had been decades—and he was going to have to listen even if he wasn't going to be happy about it. I gave a moment's thought to waiting until later as the driving was going to be hairy. But he was a good driver, and once we got out of the car, surrounded by family, the opportunity would be lost and I might not have this chance again.

As we drove up-up-up and then down-down-down, surrounded by an enormous sky, I told him about the succession of disappointments that involved him putting others first, before my brother and me. I wasn't scared or shaking. I was collected. Sticking to the facts, like I do when I'm in journalist mode.

"Dad, do you understand how your ill-conceived concerns about money corrupted my desire to introduce two women in the arts? Do you see how this might have impacted me? And Marianne? No one was trying to get anything from anyone. Do you understand how this puts whatever wackadoodle idea you have about money before an innocent networking moment orchestrated by your daughter?"

He nodded.

"It's a pattern," I told him. "You put most other people before me. Like how you handled the aftermath of the accident, keeping me from reaching out to Jenny and her family and insisting on my silence. It was the lawsuit—financials first—my feelings, second."

He nodded again, eyes still on the road.

"Do you remember when I came to Philly to talk about the accident and you fell asleep during our conversation?"

Not surprisingly, he said, "I never . . . I don't remember that. When was that?"

I just shook my head and moved on. It wasn't worth reconjuring, and I just wanted to get through this.

He was quiet. Still nodding. Nowhere for him to go but forward, zigzagging through the switchbacks.

After a few minutes, he said, "I have a lot of regrets, Ellen." He didn't elaborate, but I didn't want to push him in that moment.

"You're strong," he said. And then he paused. "Stronger than me."

I couldn't remember a time I'd ever heard such vulnerability in his voice.

Later, I knew he would forget the details of our conversation, just as he had forgotten our chat by the fish pond in his backyard. But luckily, I would remember.

REPAIRING

We can't heal what we can't feel.

—Miriam Greenspan

SPRING 2017

FOR AS LONG AS I CAN REMEMBER, I'VE KEPT A CLEAR plastic box lodged deep in the far corner of my office closet. Inside are a coverless, ringed notebook of poems that I started writing in 1967, a yellow manila envelope stuffed with letters to my grandmother, a handful of college essays, photographs from my twentieth high school reunion and the accident site from my 2006 trip, a draft of a children's story I began in 2008, and multiple rejection letters from literary publications for an essay titled "The Accident."

Why do I keep these things?

Every few years, when the house was quiet, something would pull me to that closet and I would take out the box and sit on my office floor and comb through documents, notebooks and folders. I would read some. Scan others. But on this particular day, I was rummaging with more energy and determination than usual, as if, this time, I would find something I had not yet seen.

And this time, I did. It was a set of stapled, photocopied pages. Eighteen pages. In my own preteen handwriting.

The pages were an assignment from our eighth-grade English teacher to write an autobiography. I was one month from fourteen, just about a year after the accident. On previous dives into this container, I had seen these pages and skimmed them. But as I read along this time, I remembered why I had only gotten so far. What followed from a few energetic opening lines quickly became a chirpy, teenage rendering of a life focused on parents, grandparents, friends, and pets.

It began with an epigraph, though I'm sure I wouldn't have known what that was then.

I feel secure in Daddy's sweatshirt. Those words repeat over and over in my brain. But they are gone now. I've written them down and now they are gone. I've let them escape onto the paper and they are gone. If I let the words of my life out and become words on paper, have I killed them? Have I killed my past? Have the words I use to describe myself gone? Oh, but I DO feel so secure in my father's sweatshirt. It's big and warm and I know he has worn it. I feel secure in Daddy's sweatshirt. I belong in Mommy's lap. I love to sit myself down by my third-floor windowsill and look out onto my life.

I don't remember feeling this. I don't even remember my father letting me wear it, it most likely being his Dartmouth sweatshirt, his alma mater, a place he spoke of with great fondness. But these lines reminded me of my strong attachment to my father at that age. Though I was fearful of his temper, I was a Daddy's girl. Even after the accident.

"A wonderful start!" Mr. Johnson wrote in the margin. And then, "What an experience!" "Not uncommon!" Even, "Ha!"

On page two, I read:

There I am. All thirteen years and eleven months of me. My name is common, my life is probably all-American, and to a foreigner I may just look like everybody else, but I feel ALIVE, and living is something I want to do for a long time to come.

My editor hat was now on. Why would a thirteen-year-old talk about wanting to live for a long time to come?

Perhaps because she'd had a brush with death.

Sitting cross-legged on my office floor, like a child, I made myself read every word of this tween-age document.

But when I got to the middle of page twelve, I came upon this:

> The year (seventh grade) was going easy for me until one Thursday afternoon in April of 1972, Jennifer, her sister Caroline, her mother and I had an experience that to this day (over a year later) causes great pain to their family and me.

Oh. My. God.

What followed was an account of the accident, in my own words, in my own handwriting! There, with me, in my house, in my office closet, all this time.

My body was buzzing. Electrified. Moving and still at the same time, again. I exhaled and continued reading.

> Early that Thursday morning, Jenny's mom had promised us a ride home that afternoon after sports let out.

The ride home was prearranged? I didn't remember that! I believed it was a last-minute arrangement because of the rain.

> Well, as it turned out, the weather was pretty wet and gloomy and we didn't have sports. Jenny and I decided to wait in the library for that hour until she arrived. We didn't get much of our homework done; we had been busy chattering about the play at school we wanted to see that night with Jenny's sister. Soon enough, three-thirty came and we went into the parking lot to wait for her mother.

We were picked up in the library parking lot? How was it that I could see myself standing by the field house as it began to drizzle? How could memory be so unreliable?

As we were driving up McCallum Street in Mount Airy only four blocks from my house (Caroline being in the front passenger seat, I being behind Caroline, and Jenny next to me) we stopped at the light at the corner of McCallum and Carpenter Lane. As she started up again, a large aluminum truck coming up from Carpenter Lane to the right of us bashed against the side of our VW sending us to the extreme left corner of McCallum and Carpenter. I had fallen forward hitting the front seat, not noticing for a while the great amount of blood dripping from my mouth and hands. My front tooth had been knocked entirely out. Jenny was still draped over the front seat and I put her back and her eyes were shut.

Put her back? What was that about?

Her mom was crouched to the side moaning half out of unconsciousness, half out of pain and Caroline with her knee bleeding as much as my mouth was calling for help for her mother while I, too shocked to do or say anything but cry, sat dazed and finally awoke myself enough to realize Jenny's condition and call for help.

VW, woman to Chestnut Hill...two to Chestnut Hill...one to Germantown...report to Carpenter and McCallum.

This last bit was probably what I could recall from hearing the police dispatch radio. Or, perhaps more likely, something I may have seen or heard on a television show.

I was holding tightly onto Caroline in the back seat of a police car dabbing my bleeding mouth with a wad of Kleenex someone from the crowd had handed to me while the police radio blared the directions. Caroline said to me with what was left of her strength, "Well, Ellen, I doubt very much that we will be able to see the play tonight, huh?"

"Yeah," I said, chuckling.

Then a line break, followed by the words, Chapter Three and More Growing Up.

Jenny was unconscious for five days afterward, her mother had broken collar bones and a broken leg and Caroline stayed over one night at the hospital for stitches and two chipped teeth.

It appears that I did know some of what happened after— knew and then must have forgotten.

I, on the other hand, spent the night at home but in the most uncomfortable way. From 3:45 pm that afternoon until 9 am the next day, we couldn't stop the blood from dripping out of my mouth. At the hospital, I had had x-rays taken of my neck and nose area and there was a slight sprain of my nose.

A nose sprain? I didn't remember that either. Could this explain some of my allergies?

That was not the noticeable part of my uncomfort-ableness. Grandma and Grandpa came over...

What? They were both at the house?

...and Grandma bathed me and soothed me like a

newborn baby. (And in a way I was.) I was put to bed and Grandma sat by my side until I fell asleep while my parents called the hospital to see about Jenny, Caroline and their mother.

I was relieved to read that I hadn't imagined my grandmother giving me a bath. This depiction confirmed it.

So my parents had called the hospital! Like me, they had just forgotten. How could I have been so sure that we didn't call, didn't reach out, didn't do anything?

The next morning, after a sleepless night from visible blood clots forming from my gums, we drove to the dentist. Dr. Ritter...

Wait? Dr. Ritter? Not Dr. Melman?

Dr. Ritter fixed me up so I wasn't bleeding and the rest of the day I took it easy, front toothless. In the later afternoon, we went to see Caroline; she was staying at her grandparents' house.

Whoa. We went to see Caroline? I had no memory of this. Clearly, neither did Caroline. Perhaps the memory of our check in was outweighed by a time that was turned upside down. I was surprised and very pleased to discover that we made some kind of effort to reach out.

But how could I forget that?

The police had left my book bag with Caroline's grandparents and as I looked through my undamaged books, I found my entire front tooth.

My book bag was with Caroline? Not at the police station?

Dr. Ritter said I made medical history. A tooth can

only be replaced easily back in its place within an hour after it has left the mouth. But he did a root canal and over twenty-four hours later, my tooth was back in my mouth. The accident depressed me for months after and during that time, I kept a notebook.

A root canal expert at thirteen. And there was a notebook! The desire to put all of this somewhere was so strong. A notebook I no longer had. Had I thrown it out? To honor my father's wishes to stay quiet? To keep from upsetting my mother by removing what was messy?

That feeling of almost losing an arm or a finger or losing what has become a very wonderful living experience for me; it haunted me.

Ah. So I did, indeed, sense how close I had come to death.

And knowing my disposition, I could never deal with a change in any way from the accident. I went through a phase where I felt that I lived too good of a life and soon I'll have to "pay" for it.

There was something familiar to me about this, in a raw, primitive way. I remembered struggling with the feeling that there would somehow be consequences for my lucky break. Though back then everyone told me I was lucky, I felt unlucky for having survived. I felt I would have to pay a heavy price.

The tone swiftly shifted, and the words became a philosophical preachy sermon about "the awkward age," and then, gleefully, I pulled the autobiography together with a bow.

That's me! All thirteen years and eleven months of me. I love life and the feeling of being alive—let that be known throughout my whole body and soul!

My almost-fourteen-year-old voice. In black and white. On the page. Written with my own hand. There, all the time. In my closet. Left like the breadcrumbs Hansel and Gretel used to find their way back home.

Suddenly, a sound released from deep in my diaphragm—a whole-body-heaving, breath-taking wail that had taken such a long time to come.

•

Our fortieth high school reunion was scheduled for May 2017. I booked my flight and made plans with my father, my mother, Alysse, and Marianne. And Jenny. It was time. I emailed her to make dinner plans and she swiftly agreed.

My father had been diagnosed with prostate cancer a few years before, and true to form, he hadn't once complained about pain or discomfort. But now cancer had moved into his bones. It was stage four. The progression was eerily like his father's, which also began as prostate cancer with bone metastases, from which he ultimately died. Dad was doing well, but I needed to see him for myself as he wasn't big on reporting the facts.

We met for lunch at Reading Station, and he walked so fast through the crowds I had to grab hold of his hand to keep from getting separated. His warm hand felt good. It had been a long time since I'd held my father's hand. It immediately brought back a favorite memory, my first, of being three or four. It was the early 1960s. We had briefly lived in the Chicago area when my brother and I were young. Dad and I were in a park in Deerfield in the middle of a protest. He was active in the civil rights movement, and this particular gathering was a protest against the building of a housing project that excluded people of color. We stood in a circle, his hand in mine on my left and the hand of a brown-skinned man on my right, as we sang "We Shall Overcome."

We ate a hearty breakfast at the station and, at his insistence, headed over to the Philadelphia Flower Show.

His energy was impressive. Eighty-three, his body riddled with cancer, yet he was alert, aware, and active. He was volunteering financial consulting services to a few green start-ups, reading a book a week, and staying active on his condo board. His thick jet-black hair was significantly grayer and wispier, just like his mother's, my Grandma Jane's, at his age, but he was agile. After the show, he insisted we run for the bus and walk seven blocks to his apartment in the rain to save cab fare. I think he was glad I came, but he talked less about how he felt and more about how he wished he could play tennis and eighteen holes of golf. He remained in the present tense, which I was discovering was his mechanism of survival.

•

As I passengered around Philadelphia in various Ubers and then into the suburbs visiting family and friends, the skin of my hometown city reached out and touched me again. The narrow wind of the roads, the extreme tilt of the terrain, the density of the tree line. It felt sweet to be back on Philadelphia's twisty streets and rolling hills, especially in early spring. There was such beauty in the variance of this landscape. Walking in the city, I noticed how many graveyards there are, forcing the eye down. How many of the streets still had original brick, making them wobbly to walk on, terrible for a high heel. Unlike Chicago, the variance on Philadelphia's terrain keeps the eye focused on what's right in front.

All of this was so different from Chicago, a city of skyscrapers that make you look up, take the long view. A city where the streets are flat, firm, and solid; where from the window of an airplane, you can see the actual grid of the city just like a paper map; where you can stand by a window in any skyscraper and see for miles to Indiana, even Wisconsin.

I thought about how writing didn't take hold of me until I moved away. Philadelphia was the place where I started to write about the things that were right in front of me. But Chicago was the place where I became a writer, the kind of writer who dives into things that are hidden below the surface. All of this made me wonder about the nature of place on the life of a writer.

Could the wide-open spaces of the Midwest have beckoned, making me feel safe enough to explore the hidden spaces inside? Was there more room to think in Chicago? Was the beautiful rolling landscape of the East Coast more like a writing obstruction than a writing prompt? Were there too many hidden spaces in Philadelphia that made it not feel safe? Did Chicago's wind help set my writing in motion?

•

On my way to Alysse's, where I was staying for the weekend, I made a stop at my high school to walk the campus and take photographs. I walked through the front hall where, decades ago, in between classes, we flung our canvas book bags and collapsed to the oak floor in a constant reconfiguration of teenage trios and quartets. That welcoming front hall. The switchboard was long gone, but the counter was still there as were the same thick, heavy oak table and the portraits of alumni and former headmasters on the walls. I climbed the stairs to the auditorium and poked my head into the classrooms where I took English and French. I walked out the doors where we played four square under the stone arch. I wandered by the graveyard where we all used to hang out, eat lunch, gossip, and play football.

When I walked into the meetinghouse, where for six years I spent an hour every Thursday from 10 to 11, I moved into an immediate, involuntary silence, an awed hush as I took in those long lines of oak benches with the sun-lightened, now pale-green cushions. Unlike the synagogue where I now spend much of my time, there was nothing on the windows of the meetinghouse. No curtains or blinds. No paintings or art of any kind on the walls. What happens inside is what matters for Quakers. It's something I respect and admire deeply. Quakers believe the voice of truth dwells within each of us, and silent meditation rather than a priest or pastor allows us to access it. The Religious Society of Friends doesn't rely on oath or liturgy because Quakers only tell the truth. It would be redundant. Instead, they believe we have the opportunity to be called by a God, the Divine, a Higher Source to be quaked to move from a seated position and speak that truth. The only ritual for a Quaker is a weekly silent meeting for worship. Every Thursday I sat, restlessly, with classmates, teachers, and school staff on those cushions fashioned with ties on long wooden benches, trying to empty my mind of distraction, waiting for the strength to speak, waiting to become an instrument of the Divine.

I had spent so many hours here in silence with so many people I respected, wanting to be sparked to speak. But in all of those Thursdays through middle school and high school, I never found the strength.

Ironic, I thought. Here, imposed silence was a good thing. A ritual created to be thought-inducing, even relaxing. An hour designed to return us to ourselves or the Divine. Silence that ultimately urges the words to the surface, prompting us, quaking us to speak. And yet, there's another side to silence. When imposed to keep the silence, to keep the words from coming out altogether, it can tear someone apart.

I had felt the first cuts of that ripping. But I could also feel the resistance. I was starting to feel something I understood to be a more mystical sense of God, God as the Source of a magnificent and complicated order. An order we cannot see or fully understand. But this thing we call God set this order in motion. If we pay close attention and have faith in this exquisite intelligence, we might just be able to tap into pieces of it. Every part has a different attribute or quality. We might be able to right a wrong. To revisit something from our past. To do it over. To reunite with a lost part of ourselves.

•

That night I met Alysse and Marianne in the city, followed by a sleepover at Alysse's. After her divorce, Alysse had moved into a house that better accommodated her life on wheels and was working as a landscape architect with the disability movement on accessibility projects in public spaces. She co-produced an art fair that featured painting, sculpture, photography, and jewelry made by people with disabilities and returned with more vigor now to making her own sculpture. Her work was spectacular, even more so now than when she was in high school as she had been playing with the sensuous curves and lines and twists and pulls of the human body.

Marianne was still living in Denver and had developed a painting mentoring business with workshops all over the United States. Her color-rich, textured abstracts were magnificent and were attracting commissions all over the globe. I was overflowing with love and admiration for these two women, my dearest friends, who had been through so much on their own and with me, who not only survive, but thrive. After dinner, we headed to Alysse's where we talked late into the night.

The weekend was full of parties and campus tours and conversations with people I hadn't seen in decades. It was the biggest turnout yet for a reunion, the first reunion that, for me, was all about the pure joy of reconnecting. It was a chance to see how we had grown beyond our yearbook photo to become multi-dimensional people with interesting jobs and professions, husbands, wives, partners, children, as well as express the strength and character carved into us from divorce, loss, and health challenges.

I was reminded how easy it is to forget and dismiss, how imprinted we are by the people and experiences of our early life. It was a lesson in returning, how a mere walk down that front hall again, into the classrooms and the library and the auditorium and the gym where so many character-making, micro-events occurred, could be its own reward.

•

Sunday was Mother's Day, and class reunions are always scheduled, strategically it now seems, for Mother's Day weekend. So I packed up and headed over to my mother's condo at her retirement village.

In the years since she and her boyfriend Roy had split up, we had become closer. She was making more of an effort to spend time with me and David and the girls. She traveled to Chicago once or twice a year now. I thought the time was right to try again to talk with her about the accident, especially about what I remembered after we got home from the hospital.

"Sure," she said, but her face said otherwise.

I had written my memory of the afternoon and evening of the accident, an early draft of a long-form piece I was working on. I thought it would be easiest to read what I had written to her, so I read the part just after we arrived home from the hospital that afternoon after the accident, the part that included her retreating to her bedroom and Grandma Jane's visit.

When I finished, she was still. Her eyes filled with tears, and her nose began to run. She leaned over to her bedside table to grab a Kleenex. After a minute, she said, "It's amazing, honey. Really beautiful and powerful." She had been an English major in college and was excellent at catching typos and awkward sentence structure. But I wasn't looking for her edit. I was looking for something else.

"What about the content, Mom?"

"Oh, honey," she said, dabbing her eyes with the Kleenex. "I'm just so sorry you had to go through all of that." Then she stopped talking and gazed into the distance.

It wasn't clear to me if she meant she was sorry I had been in an accident or she was sorry about how she handled things. I was tempted to ask, but her expression kept me from doing it. In her later years, she had become even more sensitive. Even in my late fifties, I still hated to upset her. So I couldn't bring myself to ask.

But her tears told me everything I needed to know. As she composed herself, I found myself tearing up too. I reached out to hug her, and we held one another for a long time.

I knew this trip would be emotional terrain. It was spring, after all.

It made me think there's always more than one spring: the one we are in and the one of our memory.

•

The following day I was in my mother's Honda Civic. Jenny's townhouse was only twenty-five miles from my mother's retirement community, but it was rush hour and Google Maps told me it would take just over sixty minutes. There was no dashboard map in my mother's car, and my cell charge was down to 12 percent from a full day's use. This trip was going to be a race against battery life. I unplugged the phone and mouthed the words to the Shema prayer, adding, please let there be enough charge to get me to Jenny's.

I refused to let a low battery stop me from dinner with Jenny. I needed to see Jenny, face to face, to tell her how deeply I regretted not reaching out after the accident, to acknowledge how frightening and terrible it was. To apologize. To tell her how horribly I felt about letting the silence come between us and our friendship and how it haunted me still. It felt like I wouldn't be able to move on without doing this, even if she couldn't forgive me. And if the moment felt right, I was also going to tell her about my plans to write about it. And if I was lucky, receive her blessing.

My heart was pounding even as I was holding my breath. I was familiar with this combination: my body moving and being still at the same time. The drumbeat of panic.

What if the phone just shut off?

I checked my iPhone. It was down to 7 percent. And I was only forty minutes in.

God, please let me arrive at Jenny's door so that I can tell her how sorry I am.

I was on ultra-octane alert at every turn, to every sound, for every fraction of a percent reduction on the battery bar, and at the holding of my breath. It was already going to be a challenging evening, why had I made it even more difficult? Was it fear? Self-sabotage?

When I pulled up in front of her townhouse, my phone was at 1 percent, just enough to tell her I had arrived. I exhaled fully for the first time in over an hour.

When she approached the car, she was walking slowly, supported by a cane. I leaned over to open the door, and she flashed a big smile.

"Hey there," she said as she approached the door.

"Hi. Do you need a hand getting in?"

"No. I'm good. Just give me a minute here." She maneuvered her cane, navigated the front seat, and leaned out to close the car door. When she settled into her seat, she said, "Let the violins play because I'm a symphony of symptoms."

I studied her face, and there it was, that smile. Which made me smile. We were both smiling. Then, laughing. Like we were twelve.

I wanted to give her a hug, but the way we were seated, the positioning wasn't quite right. We did, however, glance briefly at one another before I began to drive. She looked exactly the same, just a tad grayer and a smudge wrinklier, like me. But I saw the spark in those beautiful green eyes.

"Seems like there's a lot going on for you right now," I said, tentatively. I'm wasn't sure how much she wanted to talk about her health.

"Yeah. You don't know the half of it," she said, followed by a sigh. "But we'll get there. Let's get out of the complex first. Turn left and we'll head back toward the main street. The restaurant is close, just five minutes from here."

I was grateful for the grounding nature of practical matters like directions. In the moments between instructions, she filled me in on the headlines of her health issues. She told me how she fell at work a few years before, which injured her back and kept her from working. She also had carpal tunnel syndrome in both wrists, and, to top it off, she had recently fallen and broken her forearm.

"I'm in pain much of the time," she said in that matter-of-fact way that I remember about her, with not the slightest bit of whine in her voice.

When we arrived at the restaurant, she said, "We can park in the handicapped spot. I've got a handicapped hang permit." When she took it out of her purse and hung it on the mirror, I saw her arm brace and hand bandage.

It was a Monday night, and the restaurant wasn't busy. Just one or two tables with diners. We were seated quickly by a fawning server who escorted us to a table. He asked how we lovely ladies were doing this evening, putting on the charm, and she fired a few playful one-liners back at him. I took advantage of his friendliness to ask him if he'd watch my phone that was charging at the bar while we were having dinner.

The exchange warmed my heart. Her body might have been broken in places, but her spirit clearly was not.

My eyes were watering. I was feeling really emotional. As the minutes ticked by over dinner, I was recalling what first drew me to Jenny. Her positivity. Her humor. Her grace. The light in her eyes. I felt like a terrible person. A fair-weather friend. So many years of silence had been such a waste of precious time.

I decided then that this evening would be about my apology and a chance to hear more about her life. I wouldn't mention the writing. It was more than I could handle. I would save it for another time.

She ordered the chicken cacciatore. I wasn't very hungry, but ordered a small pasta and a salad. I wanted a glass of wine, but she didn't order one, so I decided not to, figuring it was a good idea since the drive home was already worrying me just a little.

After we talked about her work injuries and caught up on our parents and siblings, children and her grandchildren, and I shared some highlights from the reunion party, it was time.

"Jenny, I'm so glad you agreed to see me. I was concerned that you wouldn't want to."

"Oh, Ellen, I was thrilled when you wrote. Absolutely delighted that you came out all this way to see me."

I exhaled. "I can't even tell you what that means to me, Jenny. I feel like..." Already she was blurring in my sight. My eyes were flooding. I dabbed them with a napkin. "I am so ashamed at how my family responded to the accident. We didn't reach out. We didn't do what I taught my own children to do, to be there for members of your community during times of crisis. We just..."

She interrupted me.

"What do you mean you weren't there for me? You were great when I got back to school. You stood by my side like a guard, like an angel really, protecting me from everyone."

"What? I don't... But I never even came to see you at the hospital."

"Sure you did. You and Alysse. Alysse's mother brought you. I'll never forget that."

"Jenny. I have absolutely no recollection of this. Are you certain?"

"One hundred percent."

"Well, why does it feel like we never had a conversation about the accident?"

"We did at the very beginning. When I first got back to school. But then something happened over the summer. When I approached you back at school in the fall, you said you were sorry but you couldn't talk about the accident. You said it very nicely, but it struck me as very odd."

The lawsuit. I must have been told not to say anything because of the lawsuit. I was a good girl, doing what I was told.

I told her what I was thinking, that it probably had to do with my father asking me to stay quiet because of the lawsuit.

"It was quiet at my house too," she said. "I don't know if I ever told you what it was like for me after."

"I don't think we ever had a real conversation about it," I said.

"Well, I was at Germantown Hospital. My mom was at Chestnut Hill Hospital. My grandmother was taking care of Caroline. Once I came out of the coma, I was really light, down to fifty pounds. I really wanted to see my mom, but my dad told me I had to get up to sixty pounds in order to see her. They weighed me every day, and I was trying to eat as much as I could. I really needed to see my mom and make sure she was okay. I remember I was fifty-six pounds, and I put a bunch of heavy things in my pockets the next time I was weighed so I could make weight. Finally, they took me to see my mom, and I stood in the doorway of her hospital room and saw her lying in the bed, and as I approached I said, 'Mom! I'm here!' She turned her head and looked out the window. Things were never the same after that."

"Oh, Jenny. That's heartbreaking." By this time, we both had stopped eating. I was listening to her with my entire body.

"Yeah. It was rough. It was the 70s. No one talked about anything. I admire how my dad kept us all together as a family and moving forward. I had Caroline of course, but we were just trying to get through school and trying not to make waves."

"Caroline referred to it as a 'cone of silence' that came down on all of us."

"Maybe it was more like a blanket of silence," Jenny said. "Because it came from a place of protection."

I nodded. I couldn't have seen it at the time, but these words felt true now.

"Back when we talked about the accident at our twentieth reunion, you said, 'We are survivors, Ellen.'"

"Did I? Don't recall that. Sounds like something I might say." She gave me a quick smile, but then her expression shifted. "To my mind," she said, digging into her salad, which prompted me to pick my fork back up, "you actually saved my life, Ellen."

"What? Are you kidding me? What do you mean?"

"I'm serious. In two ways. You may not recall this, but at the second impact, the one with the parked car, I was slipping backward on my mother's seat, on broken ribs. You actually grabbed me and set me back upright, leaning against you."

"I did?" The words "I put her back" that showed up in my eighth-grade autobiography popped into my head.

"Yes. And your screaming helped too."

"Oh, God. How awful! I screamed? Really? Through a bloody mouth? How was that lifesaving?"

"It was. I heard you scream, 'Jenny's dead! Jenny's dead!' And my sister yelled back, 'She's not dead!' And then you shouted, 'Jenny's going to die! She's going to die!' I heard every word. I was actually concentrating on your voices. You know how when a child gets hit in the head on the field with a ball and the doctor tells you to keep the child awake, to not let her fall asleep? It was the same with me. I had a head injury, and your yelling kept me alert. I think it kept me from slipping into the coma then. It wasn't until I was placed in the ambulance that I went into the coma because I couldn't hear the voices anymore."

I put my fork down. I could no longer eat.

She was turning my world upside down, again. I had been focusing for so long on what happened between the car and the truck. I hadn't given much thought to what happened inside the car during the crash and just after, until help arrived.

The longer we spoke, the more memories were surfacing. I joked that I had opened a Pandora's box, but she insisted that the box was actually a gift. There was a way in which she, too, had been silenced. The accident wasn't a topic of discussion in her home, either. It felt good to talk, she said. Healing, even. Who better to share this with?

Then she asked, "So are you writing about it?"

I swallowed hard. I had decided not to raise the topic, and I surely didn't expect her to bring it up. She may have read a blog post where I mentioned the possibility. Or the essay I wrote for my alumni magazine about how I had tried to write the story of the accident but it hadn't gone well.

There was no reason to push the subject aside. The silence around this topic had lasted too long as it was.

"Yes. Yes, I am," I said. "I am thinking about writing a memoir about it from my own perspective. Remember when I reached out to you and Caroline to see if you were interested in being interviewed for a nonfiction book about it?"

"Vaguely, yes."

"You both declined, and I honored that, of course. The accident changed your life in far more dramatic ways than it did mine. But I realized there was a story in there that was mine too. But under no circumstances would I want to put you both through any more than you've already been through. I struggle daily with how to tell the story without doing that."

"Ellen," she interrupted. "You are a writer. You have to write it."

I wasn't sure I heard her correctly.

She pressed on. "You need to write it in your own words without any barriers. Without anyone else telling you how or what. Not even me."

"But . . . "

"No buts about it. You need to write it. To heal. Now let's get me home and you back on the road."

In the car on the way back to her house, she said she wondered if the reason she remembered so much might be to lend her memory and voice to my project. It was a very generous thought. It reminded me of the Vietnam veteran I had read about who refused to take the medication that would keep his nightmares at bay because, he said, he felt he needed to be a living memorial to his friends who died in Vietnam. Perhaps we were both living testimonials to what defined us.

When I pulled up to her townhouse, she dug around in her bag once again and handed me a piece of lined paper with her handwriting on it.

"I've been thinking about this ever since you and I have been back in touch. I wanted to see what you thought about it."

It read, "Does our past define us or do we liberate ourselves from our past?"

I promised her I would think about it. But it had been a long night. My head was swirling, and I wanted to get home safely. She nodded and we hugged, and I watched as she walked slowly down the path to her house, shaking my head, stunned into silence by her grace.

I have been thinking about her question ever since.

I'm struck by the fact that all through those post-accident school years, she and I were alone in our beds at night unaware that we were on parallel journeys that would teach us how to navigate brokenness. It was numbing. Paralyzing in ways. But it was also strength-building. You get through an experience like the one we shared, at our young ages, Jenny without her mother, and then years later, you know you are strong. Stronger than we could ever know.

Could it be this strength that pulled us back toward one another after so many years, despite so many obstacles? I don't know. But whatever it was that drew us together to break a long silence, to start the conversation we lost in the spring of 1972, gives me incredible hope.

I'm in awe of the intensity of our desire to be heard and the strength of that fragile light that stays lit between us.

EPILOGUE

GOD WASN'T RECOGNIZED IN THE HOUSE I GREW UP IN.
However, beauty was. There was a great commitment to
that. But also, on the flip side, a deep fear of brokenness.

My mother was put together, flower-fresh, almost
every day of her life until a few months before her death.
This meant color-coordinated clothing, jaunty scarfs,
handcrafted earrings. Freshly cut, colored, and curling-
ironed hair. Clean, brushed and flossed teeth. Dewy skin.
Never a mangled nail.

So when my mother, whose only health issue was anxiety,
died suddenly of pneumonia on Christmas Eve morning in 2017
at eighty-one, it not only brought intense grief but also shock.
She was completely healthy until a tooth extraction led to a
terrible reaction to an antibiotic, which led to a perfect storm
of chemistry and the pneumonia that finally took her from us.

After her death, I leaned in to the Jewish tradition of
gathering, burial, and reciting Kaddish, on which I had
become more reliant in recent years after losing my Grandma
Jane, my Grandpa Kurt, and my father-in-law. But in her will,
along with a handful of financial instructions, my mother
had two requests: She did not want a shiva, the Jewish ritual
named for the traditional seven days of mourning, and she
wanted to be cremated.

"Take my ashes somewhere beautiful," she wrote. "Say nice things about me and scatter them."

My Jewish anchors of belief showed up when my mother entered hospice. She was in Philadelphia. I was in Chicago. And my brother, San Francisco. Before she fell into the coma that would take her, my mother insisted that we not come to her bedside. It was like her to keep people from seeing her when she was not at her best, when she was a little bit broken. My brother and I had just been in Philadelphia to help her move when she fell ill with pneumonia. She had been in the ICU the entire time we were in her apartment packing boxes and organizing her things. By the time we were done, she had been moved from the ICU to a private room, and it looked like she was on the mend. At her urging, we left town.

But instead of getting better, she began to slip away, fast. We were told by hospice nurses that she could go at any time.

In my daily conversations with my brother during that exceedingly long week before she died, I struggled not to jump onto a plane to be by her side. Jews go to the sick. We sit beside them. We support them. We act as witnesses. It's a mitzvah. A commandment. We band together. We comfort one another. My Grandma Jane taught me this.

Jews know how to address illness and death.

Unless the sick person does not wish it.

My mother did not wish it. And my brother insisted that we honor her wishes.

When it had dragged into days, I went to see my rabbi. I asked her what I could do so many miles away. How to not be there? How could I bear this, Jewishly?

In our conversation, I told her that while she was in intensive care, my mother had shown brief moments of serenity when I played bossa nova tracks by Frank Sinatra and Carlos Jobim from my phone.

That's when my rabbi gave me the radical idea to alternate listening to that track as well as a chanted version of the Shema, which I did, on repeat for an entire week as my mother lay dying. In this way, I could conjure up the smile on her face, her calmed demeanor, and feel close to her.

On Christmas Eve morning, I woke up with a start and the deepest, most-other-worldly sadness I've ever felt. I knew she was gone.

In the days and weeks after that, we had to manage what remained. As it turned out, I had to go to Philadelphia just a few weeks after her cremation for Alysse's mother's memorial.

So I arranged to pick up my mother's ashes there to bring them to Chicago with me. The funeral home sent someone to hand deliver it to me, which arrived by way of a gentleman in a suit with a white cardboard box with a gold seal in a white paper bag.

Jewish tradition has us keeping the body intact and in place, carefully watched until the time of burial. There are no guidelines for moving it from place to place. We believe in the sacredness of the body that the soul leaves behind. The fact that my mother had been cremated—something not permitted by Jewish law—had me feeling off balance, like I was in someone else's story.

So it was incredibly bizarre to take my mother's cremains like luggage onto the flight back to Chicago. The only time I let her out of my sight was when she went through the airport x-ray machine. When I got onto the plane, I grabbed a bulkhead seat and put her on my lap. A flight attendant leaned over and informed me that I would have to stash my package in the overhead bin.

Out of my mouth came, "But I can't. It's my mother."

There was a chorus of "Oh" and "I'm so sorry," but still, I would have to part with it. Airline regulations. I had made enough of a commotion that someone kindly offered to change seats with me. When I shared with my seatmates that my mother was sitting with us, it made for very interesting conversation all the way back to Chicago.

But it was similarly surreal transporting her cremains on

the final leg of her trip from Chicago to California where we decided to release her. After it went through airline x-ray, in spite of the official letter from the funeral home, the box was pulled aside for further inspection leading to a similarly macabre conversation between me and airport security.

Once my brother and I decided to take her cremains to the northern California coast, a place she had always wanted to go but never got the chance, he found just the right stretch of secluded pebble beach along the Pacific Coast.

In the days before our makeshift memorial, I knew we would create a beautiful service, but I was jumping out of my skin with discomfort. Where were my grounding pieces of Jewish mourning? The dressing in dark colors. The gathering of extended family. The rabbi's calming words. The familiar comfort of a sanctuary. The car ride to the cemetery. Tossing shovels full of earth onto the coffin that's lowered into the ground. Returning home to family and friends for handwashing and more carbohydrates than any human being needs.

I was used to community in death. These rituals had become soothing to me when we said goodbye to my grandfather, my grandmother, and father-in-law.

I followed my brother slowly down the cliff and headed for the sea. It was early morning. No other people were around. The ocean was in front of us, and high cliffs protected us from behind. A gentle little waterfall spilled onto the sand that headed toward the sea. There was just the gentlest breeze. Craggy black rock formations. Black-winged birds flew overhead.

My brother lifted the plastic bag from its container and poured the chalk-white ashes that remained of our mother in a thick line on the sand. We stood silently as each foamy wave reached for her, absorbing her as she united with the ocean, and after a long silence, we began to tell her how much we loved her and why.

I selected a reading from Kahlil Gibran's *The Prophet* and recited the Kaddish. My compromise. A salve for my Jewish soul.

We stood there for a long time. Hours. Much longer, it occurred to me, than I would have been inclined to stay at a cemetery. This would be a place, I thought, to which I would want to return. Which I would do. Every year.

As the spine of her bony fragments slowly disappeared, it was impossible to deny that we were witnessing something holy. It was as if the earth was inhaling her. Taking her back. My eyes were a blur of tears, but I was riveted by the scene she seemed to have orchestrated from her death.

Was it possible that my mother was more spiritual than I thought? Could she be showing us how one might choose to return to the Source, beyond the grave?

Suddenly, two harbor seals appeared a few feet from shore, eyeing us steadily, watching us until the ocean swallowed the last dot of her. I was surprised at the thought that entered my mind. Could it be her mother and father? Showing up as witnesses? To escort her to wherever she was going next?

In the months that followed our improvised farewell, I was troubled by the image of my mother merging, solo, with the sea. My mother had been given what she wished for, but she had died alone. Even though it had been a beautiful ceremony that her children witnessed, she went into the sea alone. She may have been comfortable with it, but I wasn't.

I was plagued by whether we had we sent her off righteously, honorably.

When we returned twelve months later to that same section of beach to honor the anniversary, to be there for her *yahrzeit* where I recited the Kaddish once again, I was hoping for a sign that though our ritual hadn't been traditional, it was still good. That's when, in the distance, we saw three seals bobbing playfully, unaware of my gaze, my relief, and my gratitude.

•

A year later, as I stepped from the jetway onto the plane that would take me from Chicago's O'Hare Airport to see my father in Florida, I shifted my carry-ons to my left hand and placed my right hand, palm open, onto the smooth outer surface of the airplane and whispered the words of the Shema.

Shema Israel, Adonai Eloheinu, Adonai Echad
Baruch shem k'vod malchuto l'olam va-ed

Hear, O Israel, Adonai is our God, Adonai is One,
Blessed is God's glorious majesty forever and ever

It's the central Jewish prayer of faith in God's oneness, suggesting that a divine presence composes everything in the universe and everything is embraced in that oneness; things and thoughts, emotions and events connect. The mystics refer to it as *ein sof*, a divinity without end.

I mouthed the words so I didn't draw attention to myself. I didn't want to look suspicious in an airport while making contact with the skin of this metal bird that I trusted would stay airborne. I did this in a way that looked like I was rearranging my load or regaining my balance while I prayed that the aircraft stayed on its flight path, landed smoothly and intact.

For decades this palm-to-plane ritual has been my practice every time I board a flight, but it felt different on this particular day. I was a healthy sixty-year-old woman praying for safe delivery to see her father who very likely has never prayed a day in his life, a man who walks the beach, plays golf, reads a book a week on his balcony in Boca Raton, a man in his fifth year of fourth-stage cancer.

Many years ago, when I first placed my hands on a plane before boarding a flight, I wasn't sure I believed in God. I reached for the side of the plane in much the same way that I reached for my daughters as infants, believing that my touch was powerful enough to create some sort of protective bubble. But I knew otherwise. I knew that death could come suddenly, even in a vessel made of the strongest metal.

Praying is a leap of faith. But so is putting one's life in someone else's hands.

When I turned into the parking circle in my rental car at my father's winter residence, I saw that he had noticeably aged. It had only been seven months since we celebrated his eighty-fifth birthday in Chicago, but as I walked toward him, I could see that he was a good twenty pounds leaner. His thick hair had become quite thin. And there was little sign of his annual winter tan.

He gave me a light squeeze and a smile, never much of a hugger.

I walked as he shuffled into the lobby, onto the elevator to the two-bedroom condo he and Fran rented for the winter. He walked me to the sliding glass doors that opened onto a tile patio with a spectacular view of the bay. After I took in the view, I turned and looked at him face to face for the first time. That's when I saw the large black-and-blue mark over his left eyebrow.

"Dad, are you aware there's a huge bruise over your eye?"

"Yeah, yeah."

"What happened?"

"I fell. Tripped over that damn thing," pointing to a divot in the doorway to the patio. A very noticeable one. Anyone could easily stumble over it. There were two possible places for him to land. On the carpet or tile. Luckily he had landed on the soft carpeting.

I was reminded how unflappable he was about the physical world. Unlike my mother. Nothing in his recent fall registered as a threat to him. Accidents. Illness. Disability. He had a way of pushing it all to the side.

•

Some months later, in the midst of the coronavirus crisis, my father sent an email to my brother and me with a photo of that balcony view saying that even though he and Fran were quarantined and their beach access was gone, he was doing well and in good spirits.

"The days go in an interesting rhythm," he wrote, "with short walks and reading." There were no complaints or medical updates. Just simply, "I hope to make it through," and he signed off with "much love to you both."

His ability to stay positive in the midst of a pandemic was remarkable. It occurred to me that he was responding to it the same way he had to every difficult thing in his life. His divorces. His cancer. The accident. In all these instances, he stayed in the present tense, found the positives, and "got through."

He always got through. That was consistent. Unwavering. A quality of his on which I could always rely.

Later that spring, he and Fran boarded a commercial airplane from Ft. Lauderdale to Denver followed by a four-hour car ride to Aspen. That fall, he boarded another flight from Aspen to Los Angeles, followed by one to Hawaii, and in January of 2021, another to Florida. All of these trips, pre-Covid-vaccine.

I guess this was his version of taking a leap of faith, too.

AFTERWORD

IN THE SPRING OF 2016, AS I WAS SKIMMING THE NEWS headlines on my laptop during a year of self-imposed not-writing, two words suddenly projected themselves like a text message in my mind. Those words were: seven springs.

It was extraordinary, like no other experience I have known. Words and phrases come into my head a lot, but this felt like a true interruption, as if a voice preceded them saying, "We interrupt the headlines to bring you this important message," so that I'd have to take notice. It was as if the words fell from the sky and into an opening in my head so that they would move through my arms and hands to the screen I was holding.

Right away I knew that the words suggested more than just a number and a season.

I took the first of what would become many dives into my large collection of plastic tubs filled with journals, ringed notebooks, composition books, and loose-leaf pages—the source material of a life-long diary keeper—and speed-read through the springs of my life since our reunion conversation with Jenny twenty years before. There it was, strewn across the bright red kilim rug on the floor of my home office: Six distinct springs—1972, 1981, 1994, 1997, 2006, and 2012—in which events occurred, unplanned happenings that would change everything that came after them.

But there were only six. Not seven. Had I missed one? Suddenly, the answer revealed itself. The seventh spring, the one that would bring my fortieth high school reunion the following spring, was to come. It was the spring that I had been planning to reconnect with Jenny, to break open the silence about the accident that we shared.

This twenty-year arc, set in motion at my twentieth high school reunion with a hint of completion at my fortieth, was simply too clear-cut to ignore. My heart stirred. It had been a long time. The words offered me a way to explore the story of the accident, to lift the heavy burden of its numbing silence on me, untangle some of its mystery. To make some meaning from it.

I had written about the accident in various forms before, and the tumult it caused always stopped me from continuing. If I was ever going to write another book, I thought, it would be on writing personal narrative and not a personal narrative of my own.

But it was going to be the latter.

In that moment, for the first time since I was twelve, I had the feeling that everything was going to be okay. I had found a way to pull my face from that leather seatback in the back of that Volkswagen station wagon, free my mouth, and allow it to speak my truth. It was like a door had opened, and a strong hand was offering to securely guide me out. I was being given a chance to return to this childhood trauma, feel it, and work it out on the page.

Later I learned that seven is the number representing the natural world. In Judaism, it's the divine number representing completion.

There are seven openings of the head—the mouth, two ears, two nostrils, two eyes—the area of my body that was injured, literally and spiritually. Seven directions—left, right, up, down, forward, backward, and center—interesting since in that accident and the one that would follow, I was traveling north and ended up facing west. Seven days of creation.

Could seven be the number of springs it would take to move me from brokenness to healing?

Though I ran from it, multiple times, returning to the story of the accident ultimately felt like emergency surgery. I call it my marker story: that thing that happens that changes everything that comes after.

Writing allowed me to unpack and understand my story.

Remembering and returning gave me the gift of truth, which is far less frightening than the dark, heavy, muffling silence.

Facing it allowed me to get out from under the blanket, become lighter and more agile, able to give more of myself to the world and in a better position to see other truths and, hopefully, contribute something of value.

Virginia Woolf wrote, "If you do not tell the truth about yourself, you cannot tell it about other people."

Truth telling has reoxygenated me. It has returned my breath—my soul—so that my light, my *ner tamid*, can stay lit.

ABOUT THE AUTHOR

photo: Suzanne Plunkett

Ellen Blum Barish's award-winning personal essays have appeared in numerous publications, aired on Chicago Public Radio, and told on many Chicago-area storytelling stages. She earned a master's degree in journalism at Northwestern University, where she teaches writing. Her literary publication *Thread* earned four notables in *Best American Essays*. Ellen facilitates writing workshops and works privately with writers on personal narratives. She is the author of the essay collection *Views from the Home Office Window: On Motherhood, Family and Life* (Adams Street Publishing, 2007). She lives with her husband, David, in the Chicago area and has two grown daughters.

SHANTI ARTS

NATURE ▪ ART ▪ SPIRIT

Please visit us online
to browse our entire book catalog,
including poetry collections and fiction,
books on travel, nature, healing, art,
photography, and more.

Also take a look at our highly
regarded art and literary journal,
Still Point Arts Quarterly, which
may be downloaded for free.

www.shantiarts.com